Gender and Social Movements

Social Movements series

Colin J. Beck, *Radicals, Revolutionaries, and Terrorists*
Amy J. Fitzgerald, *Animal Advocacy and Environmentalism: Understanding and Bridging the Divide*
Stephanie Luce, *Labor Movements: Global Perspectives*
Ziad Munson, *Abortion Politics*
Jo Reger, *Gender and Social Movements*
Lisa M. Stulberg, *LGBTQ Social Movements*
David Walls, *Community Organizing: Fanning the Flames of Democracy*

Gender and Social Movements

Jo Reger

polity

First published in 2021 by Polity Press

Polity Press
65 Bridge Street
Cambridge CB2 1UR, UK

Polity Press
101 Station Landing
Suite 300
Medford, MA 02155, USA

ISBN-13: 978-1-5095-4132-4
ISBN-13: 978-1-5095-4133-1(pb)

A catalogue record for this book is available from the British Library.

Library of Congress Cataloging-in-Publication Data

Names: Reger, Jo, 1962- author.
Title: Gender and social movements / Jo Reger.
Description: Medford : Polity Press, 2021. | Series: Social movements |
   Includes bibliographical references and index. | Summary: "How to
   understand gender activism, from Women's Lib to #MeToo and trans
   rights"-- Provided by publisher.
Identifiers: LCCN 2021003009 (print) | LCCN 2021003010 (ebook) | ISBN
   9781509541324 (hardback) | ISBN 9781509541331 (paperback) | ISBN
   9781509541348 (epub)
Subjects: LCSH: Sex role. | Social movements. | Social change.
Classification: LCC HQ1075 .R4354 2021 (print) | LCC HQ1075 (ebook) | DDC
   305.3--dc23
LC record available at https://lccn.loc.gov/2021003009
LC ebook record available at https://lccn.loc.gov/2021003010

Typeset in 11 on 13 pt Sabon by
Servis Filmsetting Ltd, Stockport, Cheshire
Printed and bound in Great Britain by Short Run Press

For further information on Polity, visit our website: politybooks.com

Contents

Acknowledgments   vi

   Introduction: Integrating Gender and Social Movements   1
1 People in Movements: When Movements Focus on
   Single-Gender Concerns   22
2 Gender in Movements: What Happens in Multi-Gender
   Movements   55
3 Coming to the Movement: How Gender Influences
   Pathways to Activism   83
4 Guiding Social Change: When Gender Shapes
   Movement Trajectories   114
5 Legacies of Rise and Resistance: How Gender Sparks
   Change and Backlash   143
   Conclusion: Where Do We Go from Here?   170

Notes   184
References   185
Index   202

v

Acknowledgments

Writing a book like this one is a chance to review and remember so much of what I have read over the course of my career. Often certain scholars whom I cite or know personally come to feel like old friends and this book was a chance to renew my acquaintance. Some of them are scholars I have known and cited for years such as Verta Taylor, Leila Rupp, Nancy Whittier, Kathy Blee, Rachel Einwohner, Michael Messner, David Meyer, Suzanne Staggenborg, Judy Taylor, and Patricia Yancey Martin. Others are new acquaintances such as Tristan Bridges, Kelsy Kretschmeyer, Heather McKee Hurwitz, Miriam Abelson, Kristen Barber, and Fátima Suárez. I am so grateful for knowing you and your work. Your work is a key part of the scaffolding of this book.

Essential in writing this volume is the work I did as editor of the journal *Gender & Society*. This experience honed my understanding of gender and intersectionality and gave me the foundation and the confidence to start examining how gender and social movements intertwine. It also allowed me to cast a critical eye on social movement research and explore how gender often is left out of our analyses. I wrote this book because this is the book I wanted to have earlier in the course of my academic career. As a gender and social movement scholar I have often tried to cobble together an understanding of how each influences the other. This book was my opportunity to puzzle this out in my own way. I hope students find this useful in thinking about how the world changes through social movements as well as how the world is structured through gender.

Acknowledgments

As I finish this book, I continue to be amazed by the complexity of gender in our social world – from how it shapes us to how we rebel and seek to change gender. I find that the lens of social movements allows for that complexity to emerge.

I am also grateful to the team at Polity. I had multiple conversations with editor Jonathan Skerrett starting at the 2017 ASA meetings. I was initially unwilling to start on this project, having just completed four years with *Gender & Society*. He was very patient and, through our continued conversations, I grew excited about the project and the opportunity to bring gender and social movement research into conversation with each other. Assistant Editor Karina Jákupsdóttir was also very patient as she repeatedly checked in and kept this project on track. I am grateful for the three reviewers and their comments on an earlier version of the manuscript. Their insights helped to strengthen my arguments, deepen my discussions, and clarify the points I want to make. I am grateful for their time and attention. Despite these revisions, I am not sure I was able to satisfy Reviewer 2 completely, but I did my best and their comments made for a better book.

In regard to the actual process of writing, I am forever grateful for my writing group extraordinaire – Jennifer Law-Sullivan and George Sanders. Our weekly meetings keep me on track and, as I review the chapters in the final proofing, I can recall where I wrote them, often in the library, and often in your presence. I also thank you two for being a support group through a really difficult year of Covid and online teaching. Sometimes, I needed those venting (and laughing) sessions more than I needed to write. A very special appreciation goes out to George, who read this entire book, offered excellent revisions and settled some of my anxiety.

Finally, to my cast of characters at home – Angel and Faith. I love you both dearly. Thank you for making a home. And to my fur babies – Silvia, Cricket, and the irreplaceable Ray-Ray – you all wandered down to the basement every once in a while to check on what I was doing and sometimes sit on my lap. I appreciated your love and the writing breaks I took to go upstairs one more time to see *why* Cricket is barking at the neighbors and to see if Silvia is *really* out of food and starving, as she seems to be claiming.

Introduction:
Integrating Gender and
Social Movements

A 2017 MeToo rally in Los Angeles, CA.
Credit: Ronen Tivony/NurPhoto via Getty Images

Imagine you check your social media one morning and the hashtag #MeToo is everywhere. People you know, most of them women, are sharing stories of sexual harassment, abuse, and assault. Along with the personal posts, you see multiple news stories of prominent men in politics, business, entertainment, and the media being accused of sexual harassment and impropriety (of all degrees). The narrative in each case is similar. A man (rarely a woman) in a position of power, repeatedly used that power over a subordinate regardless of her objections. Most of these men had been engaging in these behaviors for years, some of them decades. As you watch the news coverage, it seems that as quickly as the accusations come to light, the accused is punished, losing their job and access to resources, privilege, and status. The mainstream media is full of reports, and pundits are perplexed as to the source of this tsunami of accusations. You begin to think over your own life and have a few "aha" moments of your own – A boss who stood too close; A teacher who made inappropriate comments; A romantic partner who would not listen to "no."

Emerging in 2017, the importance of #MeToo was captured later that year when *Time Magazine* named the Person of the Year – "The Silence Breakers" – acknowledging the number of women who had come forward claiming they too were victims of harassment and sexual assault by powerful, cisgendered men. The beginnings of hashtag movement can be traced back to the multitude of women who accused media mogul Harvey Weinstein of sexual harassment, assault, and rape (Johnson and Hawbaker 2019; NPR 2018). Quickly following these accusations against Weinstein, the names of prominent men (and a few women) accused of behaviors ranging from sexual harassment to rape began to snowball. The list included powerful men in politics (U.S. Senator Al Franken, U.S. Senate nominee Roy Moore), entertainment (comedians Bill Cosby and Louis C. K., actor Kevin Spacey, R&B artist R. Kelly), and business (Uber CEO Travis Kalanak). Charges of sexual assault, harassment, and rape against President Donald Trump, along with his infamous statement about grabbing women by the "pussy," also added to the moment.

#MeToo was not confined to the United States. It quickly spread with charges against prominent men across the globe in countries including South Korea, Sweden, and Egypt, all experiencing "landmark" victories for the accusers (Stone and Vogelstein 2019). Initially the hashtag was attributed to white actor Alyssa Milano; however it was later credited to long-time sexual assault activist

Tarana Burke, who coined the term "Me Too" in 2006. Reflecting on #MeToo, it is clear that this wave of accusations challenged beliefs about gendered interpersonal relations, forced a redefinition of sexual consent, and illustrated how power cannot always win the silence of victims.

For as much as #MeToo tells us about the society we live in, it is also a productive place to begin an examination of gender and social movements. First, it allows us to see how social change occurs and how social movements play a role in those changes. Second, it highlights how issues of gender can be at the core of social change efforts. Third, taking a historical view of #MeToo illustrates that what appears to be a contemporary issue has its roots in the past. Finally, the mis-crediting of the hashtag to a white actor instead of the Black woman activist who created it demonstrates the importance of looking at gender issues through the lens of race and other social identities. Using the #MeToo movement as a starting place, this book explores the intersections and interactions of gender and social movements. To untangle these dynamics, I examine how gender influences social change by exploring how it shapes participants, social change goals, and the means (i.e. tactics and strategies) by which change is sought. In other words, the who, how, and why of social change is shaped by gender, even when it is not obvious to observers and participants. To understand these dynamics, I start by defining the ways in which we understand gender.

How Gender "Sorts" Society

While the common usage of "gender" often refers to whether someone identifies as male or female (e.g. sex), theorists argue that gender is more than sex and is, in fact, embedded in society in a multitude of ways beyond the individual. Judith Lorber (1994) defines gender as a process, a system of stratification, and as a structure shaping social life. To understand the difference between gender and sex, Lorber explains that we typically are assigned a sex at birth (male or female), and due to the assignment are placed in a sex category (woman or man, boy or girl). That sex category then takes on the attributes of gender dictated by our culture, prescribing our behaviors and lifelong expectations related to our gender. Gender is a core identity for individuals, set up on the binary of woman/man or masculine/feminine. People whose gender identity and sex category are in alignment are called cisgender. People also have identities outside the binary. Identities such as gender non-binary, gender non-conforming or gender fluid are present in society with more diverse identities being articulated. However, since gender is also a structure in society (Lorber 1994), it is used to sort people into the categories, making it difficult to completely break out of the binary in all aspects of life. For example, it is a relatively recent development that some places will allow identification outside the binary on official documents such as IDs, driver licenses, and birth certificates. Gender also resides outside of the individual and is commonly assigned to traits or behaviors such as acting masculine (i.e. active, rational, instrumental) or feminine (i.e. passive, emotional, nurturing). Embedded in this binary way of seeing identities and behaviors are value judgments (e.g. it is better to be active rather than passive) as well as indications of societal power (e.g. instrumental/action-oriented actions are rewarded more than emotional/nurturing ones). This illustrates how gender is both a system of stratification, that is distinguishing, valuing, rewarding individuals who show the most prized behaviors, and a structure with gendered ideas built into the very organization of society such as the home or workplace. Overall, gender is used to sort where people "belong" and what they should "do" in a society.

As such, gendered identities shape the way an individual experiences social life. Candace West and Don Zimmerman (1987) coined the phrase "doing gender" to explore how we integrate gender into everything we do. Seen as a type of performance, gender is not only a set of behaviors (e.g. acting masculine, feminine or fluid), but is also a set of social expectations for which we are held accountable. People who step out of their "side" of the gender binary – men who act feminine, women who act masculine – can be sanctioned by others in society (Lorber 1994; West and Zimmerman 1987). As West and Zimmerman put it, we can be "held hostage" to gender's production in everyday life (1987: 126). It is important to note that with the hierarchy of gender characteristics, women can often "get away with" acting more masculine than men who do "too much" femininity. The unevenness of sanctions against these forms of "deviance" tells us that gender is, in fact, a system of inequality, operating on multiple levels of privilege and oppression (Connell 1987).

Despite having our gender evaluated in everyday life, scholars note that there are places that allow more agency and control over our "doing" of gender. For instance, Mimi Schippers (2002) argues that in the alternative hard rock community, participants engage in "gender maneuvering" that reworks some of the hierarchy embedded in their interactions and contributes to an alternative gender order, while not completely eradicating it. Tony Silva (2016) found that a group of rural men who identified as heterosexual also engaged in sexual practices with other white, masculine, heterosexual, or secretly bisexual men. Silva labels this "bud sex" and notes that men continued to define themselves as masculine and heterosexual, despite having same-sex sexual encounters. In other words, they controlled the gender discourse around their behavior. Overall, despite being held accountable for doing "appropriate" gender, people can find ways to resist and change how they "do gender," to some degree.

In addition to "doing" and learning our gender, we also "determine" the gender of others. Laurel Westbrook and Kristen Schilt (2013) note that in social interactions, we draw on visual and behavioral cues to determine an individual's gender category. However, Westbrook and Schilt problematize this process by noting how transgender individuals in public settings can confuse this process and cause "gender panics." These panics are particularly apparent in spaces that are gender segregated such as public restrooms. Westbrook and Schilt remind us that even when binary-focused ideas of gender identity are changing, core beliefs in a dichotomy of sex, gender, and sexuality are still maintained. Gender then is not only something we do throughout our days, but it also something that is determined about us, based on the cues we provide through dress, behavior, and social context.

Returning to the idea that gender is a structure as well as a process, we can see how gender is present in large-scale structures and processes, such as in institutions, organizations, societal norms, and ideologies. Joan Acker (1990) noted how gender is integral in the construction of organizations, shaping policy, practices, and infrastructure. While she notes that feminist sociologists have examined male dominance in leadership, hierarchy, and opportunities in organizations, missing is a sense of how gender is embedded in the documents and policies that construct the organization and become the groundwork for its belief system. She writes that "advantage and disadvantage, exploitation and control, action and emotion, meaning and identity, are patterned through and in terms of a distinction between male and female, masculine and feminine" (1990: 146). For example, considering gender as a structure includes understanding how it shapes the division of labor, wages, performance evaluations, and job descriptions within the workplace (Martin 2003; Ridgeway 2001). These differences are not due to innate differences between women and men but instead are the result of gender positioning people differently in the social structure (Lorber 1994).

Barbara Risman (2004) adds to our understanding by arguing that it is best to conceptualize gender as an overall structure that is found in the individual level (through processes such as socialization and the construction of selves), the interactional, cultural level (evident interactions around status, bias, and power), and the institutional domain (which accounts for organizational practices, legal regulations, resources, and ideology). This conceptualization captures the complex ways in which gender exists in society with multiple levels extending from the individual, sustained in interaction, and embedded in the ways the social structure, institutions, and organizations function. Drawing on this multi-level conception of gender allows us to see how the #MeToo movement is more than just the result of the actions of individuals but is also the result of gendered interactions that are supported within organizations and structured by gendered policy, norms, and regulations. For instance, Weinstein was able to escape any sanctions for his behavior due to the institutional order he was embedded in, the power he held over those lower on the hierarchy, and laws and policies that have limits in terms of enforcement. His behavior was also supported by a culture that accepted and encouraged his domination over women.

How gender binary sorts society is also illustrated in the Weinstein case. Much of the power and control evident in his assaults were derived from his status as the most powerful person – masculine, manly, male – in the room. The power and status he achieved outside the room were also a benefit of masculinity in society. In other words, Harvey Weinstein was not just a *bad* person, he was a person, because of the divisions of masculinity and femininity in society, who was able to dominate, control, and assault women. Overall, the gender binary divides all levels of gender from the individual to the societal. In many societies the gender binary is accepted because it aligns with Western thought's use of dichotomies to understand the social world. Dichotomies divide the world into simple binaries, such as black and white, rich and poor, men and women, and in the process solidify one side's power and value in society. Our cultural aversion to ambiguity makes it difficult to see past binaries and recognize that a more complex situation exists. Therefore, the gender binary structures and sorts our world, even when people identify as being outside of it.

In sum, acknowledging that gender is multi-dimensional and always in flux contributes to how we understand the social world around us and how it changes. Understanding gender as a form of power and control in society is also key in social change. Knowing that society is always changing also helps us to understand what social movements are and how they arise.

How Social Movements Change Society

We know that social change happens in a variety of ways and is sometimes unintentional – for example, shifts in societies occur when new economies, populations, and/or technologies are introduced. However, sometimes social change is intentionally sought and can be the result of social movements. Social movements are made up of individuals who come together in organizations, communities, and/or networks with the goal of making or resisting change happening in society (Tarrow 1998). What makes these "social movements" versus other efforts to change society is that they are in opposition to some segment of society. Aspects of society targeted by social movements include the powerful elites who control institutions and the rules, laws, or cultural norms that disadvantage a societal group. Some social movements challenge the state working to change laws or policies. For instance, movements on both sides of the abortion debate work to change the laws around access to abortion with a focus on the Supreme Court, as well as on state laws. Social movements also challenge cultural ideas and work to change social norms. For example, some participants in the women's movement in the 1970s sought to change the language used to refer to women, arguing that calling women "girls," "chicks," or "foxes" was denigrating (Mallinson 2017). Overall, social movements are about changing the social order, which entails personal as well as collective change, and cultural as well as institutional transformation. For example, the lesbian, gay, bisexual, transgender, queer, and beyond movement (LGBTQ+) not only worked to change laws but also to change social norms around the acceptance and portrayal of LGBTQ+ people and worked to create a sense of pride versus marginalization in individuals. In either case – the focus on institutions or the focus on culture – the key to understanding social movements is that they are not spontaneous but are often the result of generations of organizing. Social movements are also not chaotic but instead have some sort of organizing structure, which can often vary depending on the beliefs and goals of the organization. As such, social movements can survive for long periods of time and engage multiple generations of activists (Reger 2012; Rupp and Taylor 1987; Taylor 1989; Whittier 1995).

To achieve their goals, social movements draw on a variety of actions called tactics. Those tactics can range from large-scale demonstrations such as marches on Washington, to the more individual such as legislative lobbying. Tactics can also be more symbolic and use everyday actions such as embracing an activist identity in daily life, through actions such as recycling or wearing a T-shirt connected to a movement. Movements often draw on more than one tactic, in what social movement scholars call a "tactical repertoire" (Taylor and Van Dyke 2004). Important in the creation of that repertoire is the overall strategy, or plan of action, embraced by the movement activists. For example, if the movement adopts the strategy of non-violence as the means to achieve their goals, the corresponding tactics would include those that endorse non-violent civil disobedience such as sit ins or street theater.

Strategy and tactics emerge from individuals' interactions within the movement, along with the sense of being a united group sharing a set of common values and interests. Identified as a collective identity (Melucci 1989), this sense of belonging emerges from the construction of a sense of who "we" are as a group, as opposed to "them," the opposition or target. This shared activist identity emerges from three processes: the development of a group consciousness with common values, beliefs, and goals, the delineation of boundaries between "us" and "them," and the negotiation across those boundaries in pursuit of the overall goal (Taylor and Whittier 1992). The creation of collective, or activist identities, is essential in sustaining movements and directing the course of action.

While we often think of social movement dynamics as face-to-face interactions, like the rest of society social movements moved into new dimensions on the internet. Social movement scholars turned their attention to virtual activism as the internet grew. For example, Alan Schussman and Jennifer Earl (2004) studied "strategic voting" in the 2000 U.S. presidential election. Websites popped up that allowed individuals to coordinate their votes, ensuring that "blue" or largely Democratic states would go to Al Gore, while allowing left-leaning, third-party voters to cast their ballots for Ralph Nader. The overall goal was to keep George Bush from the presidency. While the overall goal of strategic voting failed, the political activism on the internet caught the attention of researchers. Schussman and Earl coined the label "e-movements" to identify this new terrain for activism. Despite the fact that the term "e-movements" didn't catch on; the internet is now the home to much social movement activism. Activists use the internet to recruit, educate, and advocate for actions either online, such as e-petitions, or to attend in-person events and demonstrations. The lines between virtual and in-person spaces for activism often becomes blurred. For instance in 2011 when Occupy Wall Street – a social movement focused on income and wealth inequality – emerged, it focused on in-person encampments as a main tactic but also had a lively internet presence through the more than 1,500 Facebook pages established across the globe (Gaby and Caren 2015). As platforms such as Instagram, Facebook, and TikTok are developed, activists find a way to move into those spaces.

While websites and other digital spaces connect activists and serve as virtual organizing areas, hashtags promote issues and topics and connect people through subject matter. Hashtag activism results when # is added to a phrase or word as a way to spread a message or topic key to a movement, usually done through Twitter. The scenario at the start of this chapter – #MeToo – is an example of hashtag activism that is linked to a larger social movement. Hashtags organize social media content by allowing people to search for particular topics and notifying them on what is trending. Indeed, young people often turn to their social media instead of more traditional outlets for news. One of the most influential hashtags to develop is #BlackLivesMatter (BLM), which was tweeted in 2013 and became the label for one of the largest protest cycles in U.S. history. As #MeToo and #BLM illustrate, social media can be the impetus for the start of social movement organizing and protests. The United States has been the site of campaigns and movements sparked by a single tweet such as #MeToo and #BLM but hashtags play a global role as well. Examples of this include #ArabSpring and the uprisings in Tunisia, Morocco, Syria, Libya, Egypt, and Bahrain, #StopFundingHate, a pro-immigrant campaign in the U.K., and #BringBackOurGirls, a campaign to return kidnapped girls to their families in Nigeria. Overall, "[The internet] speeds up the processes of organizing and network building, creates and nourishes communities across geographic divides, and introduces new tactics and strategies" (Crossley 2017: 127).

Scholars of social movements often view their work through theoretical lenses that provide explanations for movement origins, goals, and outcomes. Those frameworks often take different views of what movements need to emerge and achieve their goals. Resource mobilization theory argues that social movements emerge when organizations and groups are able to accumulate the resources they need to build an infrastructure to support the mobilization of activists (McCarthy and Zald 1977; Jenkins 1983). The political process lens views social change as emerging when there are openings or opportunities in a society. Called "opportunity structures," these openings allow movements to emerge at times that are optimal, despite historical and long-lasting long-term experiences of discrimination or prejudice (Tilly 1978; McAdam 1982; Tarrow 1998). Scholars also argue that when one movement emerges, it often can foster other movements. Through what are called "cycles of protest," movements can interact with each other sharing ideas, tactics, and organizations, and consequently create more protest opportunities (Meyer and Whittier 1994). Another approach used by scholars is to examine the ways in which identities and group cultures are important to social movements. This perspective illustrates how being engaged in social movement communities is meaningful to the individual, sustaining activism (Buechler 1990; Taylor and Whittier 1992). Finally, the contentious politics approach views social movements as made up of public protest events such as demonstrations and sees movements as connected to other forms of collective action such as unions, strikes, and revolutions (McAdam, Tarrow, and Tilly 2001). These different frameworks tell us that the study of social movements, similar to the study of gender, examines social movements from all levels and asks a variety of questions making more complex (and interesting) answers.

How More Than Gender Matters

Any discussion of gender and social movements needs also to include a discussion of intersectionality. Often credited to Kimberlé Crenshaw (1991), and emerging from the work of Black feminist activists and scholars, intersectionality is the idea that we are a complex combination of social identities that need to be considered in relation to each other (Combahee River Collective 1978; Deborah King 1988; Patricia Hill Collins 1990). Black feminist theorists conceptualized race, class, and gender as interlocking systems of oppression, forming a "matrix of domination" in which one social identity cannot be understood completely without considering all aspects of a person (Collins 1990). This matrix of identities influences our interactions, opportunities, and access to resources (Collins 1990; hooks 1989). Intersectionality was conceived through the work of U.S. Black feminist theorists to address the racism, classism, and homophobia of the women's movement with the goal of dismantling the concept that all women experience society in the same way – or "universal womanhood." In particular, Black feminists argued that they could not be understood as either Black or women but as both. They argued for understanding people as *both/and* as opposed to *either/or*. The concept of intersectionality is key in much of the research on gender, allowing scholars to conceptualize people as more than just a gender category. Instead, scholars explore the ways in which other social identities such as race and class influence how people experience gender.

The use of intersectionality in gender theory is important to the study of social movements. A singular focus on gender in movements does not adequately capture the dynamics of gender, race, and class (among other social identities) for people engaged in social movements and how this intersection of identities shapes their experiences. An intersectional perspective also allows for an examination of how political resources and access to power varies by social groups. By not treating all social movement participants as equal in their ability to mobilize resources and influence political elites, intersectionality as a lens can examine the impact of gender along with race, ethnicity, class, sexuality, and religion (among other categories) when considering social inequality. In the chapters that follow, I present research that often examines only gender and social movements, and then work to complicate these views with an intersectional perspective.

How Gender and Social Movements Intertwine and Influence Each Other

This chapter then raises the question – Why is this combination of gender and social movements important? There are three key reasons to combine the study of gender with social movements. First, the study of social movements has been slowly integrating gender scholarship, expanding our ability to see complexity of social change efforts. Understanding that gender is more than an individual quality allows for a greater grasp of inequality and efforts to address it. Second, since gender is a system of stratification, integrating it into social movements scholarship allows for new insights into the nature of inequality and social change. As we will see, gender inequality can be the start of a social movement, as well as shaping how people experience social movements. Third, as social movements seek to change society and gender norms are constantly in flux, the integration of gender and social movements captures the dynamic of how societies change over time. I address each of these – integrating scholarship, intersectionality, studying social change – in more detail.

Integrating scholarship

Over three decades ago, Judith Stacey and Barrie Thorne (1985) argued that gender was the "missing revolution" in sociology. Doug McAdam (1992) echoed their call, focusing on social movements and asking scholars to consider gender as a factor in movements. Since the 1990s, social movement studies have begun to answer that call with an increase in gender scholarship, particularly focusing on women in movements. Feminist scholars argued that all social movements, regardless of whether or not they agitate for gender equality, operate within gendered institutions and settings and are engaged in the social construction of gender. This scholarly progress has come in two waves, with the first focused on understanding women's social movement activism (Whittier 2007). However, as gender scholars expanded their research beyond the study of women, the second wave began. It was then that scholars began to consider the topic of masculinity and intersectionality in all movements.

As a result, gender scholarship has expanded social movement theories. For example, Judith Gerson and Kathy Peiss (1985) detailed how a gendered identity is formed through the development of a gender consciousness, the negotiation of gender boundaries and the interaction with "the other." Verta Taylor and Nancy Whittier (1992) drew on this scholarship to illustrate how activist identities are created within movement communities and how they are constantly being constructed as the external environment, and group norms, beliefs, and goals shift. Relatedly, scholars have drawn on the dynamics of women's movements to advance theorizing on social movements in general (Reger and Taylor 2002; Taylor and Whittier 1995; Staggenborg and Taylor 2005; Taylor 1999). Studies of the U.S. women's movement have shaped social movement theory in multiple ways. Investigations of feminist culture prompted new understandings of movement continuity and change. Scholars of feminism articulated important concepts for all social movements, such as the existence of multiple activist identities, distinctive movement cultures, and networks of activists not visible to mainstream society. All of these concepts moved the study of social movements away from a strictly structural and resource-focused analysis. This was brought in part by feminist activists studying the movement around them, a dynamic seen in other movements such as the student, anti-war, peace, and anti-nuclear movements. In studying the movements around them, feminist researchers could also see how a movement could shape society, and how, as gender issues shifted in movements, so did the focus and goals of movements. In sum, the study of a gendered social movement such as U.S. feminism has influenced the social movement theories and concepts that can be applied to all social movements.

Addressing inequality

In addition to integrating the study of gender and social movements, studying gender within social movements allows for an investigation of a system of inequality. Even when the movement is not specifically organized around gender, gender stratification is present in movements, shaping who has power and resources. Raewyn Connell refers to this structural inequality as "gender regimes" (1987: 120) built into an institution or organization. These regimes establish who has power and who does not. Verta Taylor calls the ideology underlying these regimes "gender logic" even when they do not draw specifically "on the language of femininity and masculinity or of gender contention" (1999: 21). Taylor offers the example of "beloved community" during the civil rights movements as an illustration of how a movement not focused specifically on gender used a language of care and concern in its understanding of the social movement community. These gender regimes and gendered logics reflect the larger society and by examining them we can learn about the society in which movements form and some of the ways in which gender inequality manifests itself.

Studying social change

Studying the relationship between gender and social movements is also an investigation of how social change occurs. When social movements focus on gendered issues, such as the men's rights movement discussed in Chapter 1, gender norms and societal understandings of gender can shift. However, shifts in society, such as in the economy and labor market as well as social disruptions of war or global pandemics, can alter gender norms and spur social movement activism. For example, many African women's movements started out as peace and anti-war movements and became gender-focused movements (Tripp 2017). Here we can see how the end of the wars often brought social reorganization and a call by activists for reforming society. In the course of pressing for reforms, women peace activists also experienced political openings that "helped foster new women's activism, which sped up processes of women's rights reform" (Tripp 2017: 46). There is a consistent pattern across time and place in which movements focused on non-gendered issues give birth to gender-focused movements.

Focusing on gender inequality and dynamics of social change leads us back to the example of the #MeToo movement. Gender norms and expectations, particularly around expressions of sexuality and expectations, can result in the identification of a problem, such as sexual harassment and assault, that spreads through society. Understanding these problems as more than individual issues but as inequality embedded in societal norms can lead to the formation of a social movement. This problem, or as social movement scholars call it a "grievance," is articulated by social movement participants, diffuses into society and is embedded in activist networks. Sparked by an event, such as the highly publicized case of Harvey Weinstein, experiences are reexamined, stories are told, activists are organized, and a societal shift begins. In sum, in the #MeToo movement, a societal issue moves from being an accepted norm to a social problem and then a grievance articulated through a social movement. Through sustained attention by activists, combined with shifting social attitudes, we see that though the emergence of #MeToo can appear spontaneous and somewhat puzzling, it is instead an outcome of a movement that drew on and redefined what it means to experience sexual assault and harassment through an analysis of gender. In all, combining gender and social movements provides us with a lens to understand the world around us.

Organization of the Book

To investigate these dynamics, this volume moves from examining how the sex and gender of participants shapes a movement, to gender as an ideology or social logic shaping movements and ends by exploring reactions and responses coming from gendered movements. In doing so, Chapters 1 through 4 focus on how the gender and sex binaries – male/female, woman/man, feminine/ masculine – influence movements and activists. Since these binaries are a primary "sorting" mechanism in society with the potential to position people in certain ways, movements often reflect these binaries. However, examining how movements align themselves to these binaries does not mean that only the identities of women and men and males and females have been involved in movements. On the contrary, reviewing social movements can illustrate how non-binary, gender fluid, transgender, and intersex people are present and influential in movements. In Chapter 5, I take up some of these histories to illustrate the diversity of gender and sex identities in movements and how as understandings of gender change, so do the focus and goals of movements. My goal in this text is not to center the focus on cisgender activists but to take a broader view of how gender as a social logic organizing our lives is incorporated into social movements.

Throughout the book, I also bring a focus to what an inter-sectional perspective can bring to our understanding of social dynamics. I do so to note how identities beyond gender such as race-ethnicity, age, social class, religion, nationality, and other social identities also act as "sorting mechanisms" in society and intertwine with gender. I bring in this intersectional perspective to remind the reader of these forces and have included sources such as websites and books that will allow further investigation. At the start of each chapter, I introduce a vignette from a social move-ment and use that vignette to illustrate the concepts and dynamics of each chapter.

Chapter 1 – People in Movements: When Movements Focus on Single-Gender Concerns – considers how movements are shaped by participants' gendered concerns. Here I examine how (mostly) single-gender movements work to change or resist change of soci-etal gender norms. This chapter focuses on women's and men's movements and how they arise, what they focus on, and how they shift over time. I show how single-gender concerns can take a multitude of approaches with movement activists sometimes working in opposition to each other.

Chapter 2 – Gender in Movements: What Happens in Multi-Gender Movements – examines how gender shapes social movements that are not specifically organized to change gender norms and addresses how gender organizes movements containing multiple gender identities. Drawing on the ways in which societal gender norms sort people often into the binary, I examine how men and women can fare very differently from each other in the same movement. Here I show how participants in social movements bring their gendered understandings of the world into movements and act on gendered assumptions, expectations, and beliefs. I examine how gender shapes who is thought to be an activist and their abilities in movements.

In Chapter 3 – Coming to the Movement: How Gender Influences Pathways to Activism – I continue to draw on the dominant gender binary as a sorting mechanism to explore the different routes and processes by which people join and become active in social movements. How people come to movements is a core question for social movement scholars, and in this chapter I focus on how movements connect to people and how they convince people to join the movement as well as how people move from interested participants to activists. Just as people live gendered lives and are shaped by gendered constraints and expectations, the processes that bring them into social movements are also gendered. I end the chapter by discussing how emotions are central to all these processes and are again often shaped by understandings of the gender binary.

Chapter 4 – Guiding Social Change: When Gender Shapes Movement Trajectories – examines some of the key aspects of how social movements determine their course of action – through leaders, strategies, and tactics. As participants in movements draw on their understandings of gender, they also shape who is identified as a leader and how they lead. The work on the civil rights movement is particularly important here with feminist researchers identifying how women have led even if they weren't identified as doing so. Shaped by the people within them, movements, strategies, and tactics often draw on conventional ideas of femininity and masculinity as well as transgressing them in the work for social change. I conclude by noting that some gendered strategies and tactics are hidden, and only emerge when viewed through a gender lens.

In Chapter 5 – Legacies of Rise and Resistance: How Gender Sparks Change and Backlash – I examine how gender identities shift and develop in society and how some work to resist those changes. Here I examine how gender as a personal identity does not always align itself to the binary. I start by examining some of the tensions around gender and same-sex marriage and then examine how trans, gender non-binary, and gender fluid people move beyond the binary and how social movements have played a role aiding those identities as well as resisting them. I then explore how challenges to conventional gender norms bring backlash and countermovements seeking to undo the changes. This resistance to undoing aspects of gender illustrates once again its power in shaping society. The final chapter – Conclusion: Where Do We Go from Here? – draws on the case of the Grandmothers of the Plaza de Mayo to examine the multiple ways that gender intertwines in social movements as illustrated throughout the book. The story of these grandmothers, *abuelas*, in Argentina, highlight the key themes of this book. Drawing on their status as grandmothers, the activists illustrate how gendered people organize in (largely) same-sex movements and draw on gendered networks, identities and ideas to organize protest. They drew on a strategy that infused non-violent protest with norms of chivalry toward the elderly and women. They were able to continue their protests because of gendered stereotypes about women and those stereotypes kept their movement alive. Overall, the Grandmothers of the Plaza de Mayo and their activism serves as a powerful example of the intertwining of gender and social movements. I conclude by noting where more research and attention is needed as scholars continue to intertwine gender and social movements.

Sources to Explore

Collins, Patricia Hill. 1990. *Black feminist thought: Knowledge, consciousness, and the politics of empowerment.* Boston, MA: Unwin Hyman.

Connell, Raewyn. 1987. *Gender and power: Society, the person and sexual politics.* Stanford, CA: Stanford University Press.

Fisher, Dana. 2019. *American resistance: From the women's march to the blue wave.* New York: Columbia University Press.

Kantor, Jodi, and Megan Twohey. 2019. *She said: Breaking the sexual harassment story that helped ignite a movement.* New York: Penguin.

Lorber, Judith. 1994. *Paradoxes of gender.* New Haven, CT: Yale University Press.

Lucal, Betsy. 1999. What it means to be gendered me: Life on the boundaries of a dichotomous gender system. *Gender & Society* 13: 6 (December): 781–797.

Vegh, Sandor, Michael D. Ayers, and Martha McCaughey (eds.) 2003. *Cyberactivism: Online activism in theory and practice.* New York: Routledge.

Westbrook, Laurel, and Kristen Schilt. 2014. Doing gender, determining gender: Transgender people, gender panics, and the maintenance of the sex/gender/sexuality system. *Gender & Society* 28: 1 (February): 32–57.

Questions to Consider

1. Define what sociologists mean by gender and how it is a part of the social structure.
2. What does it mean to be held accountable for our gender? How can this process of policing gender give rise to social movements?
3. What are some of the perspectives on how social movements form? What seems necessary for this to happen?
4. What social movements are happening in your community?

In the world? Can you see how gender is an aspect of these movements?
5. What is the relationship between gender, social movements, and inequality?

Reflection

What are some of the ways in which you have experienced gender inequality? Do you feel as though there are movements that address these experiences?

1

People in Movements: When Movements Focus on Single-Gender Concerns

Protesting the Miss America Pageant on the Atlantic City Boardwalk
in September 1968.
Credit: Bev Grant/Getty Images

ATLANTIC CITY, September 7 (1968) – Women armed with a giant bathing beauty puppet and a "freedom trash can" in which they threw girdles, bras, hair curlers, false eyelashes, and anything else that smacked of "enslavement," picketed the Miss America Pageant here today.

The women pickets marched around the Boardwalk outside Convention Hall, singing anti-Miss-America songs in three-part harmony, carrying posters deploring "the degrading mindless-boob-girlie symbol," and insisting that the only "free" woman is "the woman who is no longer enslaved by ludicrous beauty standards."

They also denounced the beauty contest's "racism" (since its inception in 1921, the pageant has never had a Black finalist), and announced boycott of the sponsors (Pepsi-Cola and Toni and Oldsmobile) and refused to talk with males (including male reporters).

"Miss America pageant picketed by 100 women."
Charlotte Curtis, Special to the *New York Times*
(September 8, 1968, p. 81)

This protest, by the organization New York Radical Women, a part of the women's liberation branch of the U.S. women's movement, was to become the source of many myths and misconceptions in the years to come, in part because it received extensive press coverage, such as the above special report in the *New York Times*, the day after the protest. The biggest misconception to emerge from the protest was the characterization of the activists as "bra burners," a stereotype of feminists that still lingers today. In reality, the activists did toss items such as bras and girdles into a "freedom trash can," but without a permit to start a fire, nothing was burned. According to activist Karla Jay who was at the protest, another myth was that the activists didn't talk to men (1999). Single-gender movements, particularly women's movements, have repeatedly been the source of negative myths and stereotypes. In the case of U.S. feminism, New York Radical Women were viewed as anti-male, hence the myth of not speaking to male reporters; and too radical, as encapsulated in the myth of "bra burners." While negative, there is some truth in these stereotypes of feminists. Radical feminists, such as the ones at the Miss America pageant, rejected the norms of hyperfemininity (i.e. excessive or extreme femininity) around dress, appearance, and demeanor. These young women specifically rejected the expected foundation garments – bras, girdles, hosiery – that defined women's shapes and styles in earlier decades. In doing so, they also were rejecting the idea of beauty contests where women were valued solely for their appearance (reflecting their value to the larger society). To illustrate the demeaning nature of being valued only for beauty, activists paraded a sheep to demonstrate how women were judged like animals at a county fair. Naomi Wolf (1990) later called this the "beauty myth," the idea that no woman can ever achieve or maintain cultural norms of feminine beauty. Wolf argued that trying to achieve this goal cost women time, energy, and resources that could be used for other more meaningful pursuits. By tossing girdles and bras into a "freedom trash can," activists rejected the control over their bodies, and by crowning a sheep "Miss America" they symbolically critiqued traditional femininity as passive and controllable.

While it is easy to assume that this was just a small group of activists and a one-time protest, these women were part of a larger, more complex women's movement focused on gender inequality. Indeed, historian Alice Echols (1989) argues that it was this demonstration that brought the emerging movement with all its factions into the public sphere. The U.S. women's movement, which emerged in the late 1960s and early 1970s, was a complex movement with divisions by race, age, status, and most importantly, the focus on what needed to be changed in society. Taking the example of the Miss America protest, the women participating were predominantly white, young, college-educated, and with a history of being involved in student and anti-war protests. Overall, the history of the movement is one of political, social, and racial divisions that brought some avenues of change, collaboration, and often discord. Indeed, even the participants at the Miss America protest debated on the direction of their actions.

The Miss America protest, with its focus on gender norms and its connection to a larger movement, serves as an example of how people in predominantly single-gender movements specifically address what they perceive to be inequality. Here, gender is the source of movements, and they are often organized to change gender socialization, constraining gender norms and the resulting barriers by focusing activism on the societal institutions that uphold them. The Miss America protest, seen in the context of the larger movement, also illustrates an important dynamic of single-gender movements – where, how, and why of social change often varies widely between groups in the same movement. These differences are often forged from variations in age, race-ethnicity, education level, social class, as well as a myriad of other social identities and experiences. Overall, the work of achieving gender equality is rarely accomplished with a single collective mindset. An intersectional perspective reminds us that people experience the world differently due to their social statuses; the same is also true of their experiences and goals in social movements.

Because gender as a binary organizes and sorts people into two opposite categories (woman/man, feminine/ masculine) in society, large numbers of people in a category can experience the same constraints due to gender and come to identify them as problems. Grievances are the personal troubles that people come to identify as social problems stemming from inequality. However, griev-ances alone are not sufficient to start a movement. Lots of people can identify the personal problems they experience, but do not consequently join social movements. Grievances need a push, or opening, in the political and cultural environment to translate them into activism. As such, grievances can exist for long periods of time without a movement emerging. For example, across the world women have been denied the right to vote for much longer periods of time than suffrage movements have been organized.

However, the articulation of grievances is essential to movements. They can serve as a common bond among participants, focus the goals and actions of leaders, and serve to recruit others to the move-ment. We can see this process of identifying gendered grievances most clearly in single-gender movements such as men's or women's movements. While men have been a part of women's movements and vice versa, the focus of these movements is on addressing issues arising from gender norms around masculinity or femininity, along with the perception that these norms are the source of gender ine-quality. So, if acknowledging grievances around gender norms is not enough to start a movement, then what is?

Holly McCammon and her co-authors argue that the acknowl-edgment of gender discrimination is not enough to start a movement. Instead they argue that "gendered opportunity structures" are also necessary for these types of movements to emerge (McCammon et al. 2001). A gendered opportunity structure is an opening in the social, political, or cultural environment that allows for a movement to form. Often this window of opportunity is a matter of timing where ideas about gender in society fluctuate enough, allowing people to find each other and organize. McCammon and her colleagues base this argument on their study of suffrage efforts in the United States. They find that it is not enough to want to right a wrong, such as being denied the vote, but that society has to be open to the challenge for change. They explain, "... changing gender relations altered expectations about women's participation in the polity, and these changes in gendered expectations increased the willingness of political decision-makers to support suffrage (2001: 51). Here it is the support of decision-makers that opens up the political system and allows activists to organize. In the case of the Miss America protests, feminists were able to draw attention to their claims about women's oppression largely due to being in a period of time where there was media interested in the emerging feminist movement and members had developed media contacts to call upon. Without an open opportunity structure, activists can struggle in vain to make change and recruit others to the cause.

Much of the research on single-gender movements examines people through the gender binary of man/woman and masculine/feminine to understand how the participant's gender category influences social movements. Although this ignores individuals outside the gender binary, feminist scholars pioneered this work by acknowledging that gender differences between men and women exist. They noted that ignoring gender doesn't make activists and movements gender neutral. Instead when gender is not examined, men become the "default human" and women become the "other" in social interactions. Examining gender also captures how men and women occupy different positions in society and have different access to resources, power, and opportunities. This reliance in research on the cisgender binary of women/men, masculine/feminine, has been rightly critiqued by contemporary gender scholars investigating how trans and non-binary individuals fare in and create movements. Yet to understand how gender sorts society and creates inequality, it is important to examine single-gender movements and the way they seek to change gender. In this chapter, I explore how movements specifically organized around a gender take into consideration how gender is a process through socialization, that structures in society through institutions like the family or government, and stratifies the private and public spheres of society. I first focus on a history of U.S. feminism and then discuss how women's movements form differently around the globe.

U.S. Women's Movements

The U.S. women's movement is a productive site to investigate how movements can organize around a specific set of gender concerns and how movements can be divided on avenues to social change. Throughout its history, the U.S. women's movement centered on issues around women's roles in society, often arising from other movements. Historically, organizers for women's rights have found themselves in a pattern of being marginalized or shut out of other movements, and then regrouping to organize around their experiences as women. Taking a broad view, throughout the movement's history, women's rights activists have focused on changing gender norms and socialization, breaking down the limits placed on women by societal structures and addressing the inequality women experience as a result of gender stratification. In each stage of the movement, those goals have shifted as the movement progressed and, at times, experienced backlash and countermovements.

Early movement

The early movement emerged in the 1800s with a key moment being when Lucretia Mott and Elizabeth Cady Stanton, white, educated, upper-class women, organized the Seneca Falls Women's Rights Convention on July 14, 1848. It was organized, in part, because women had been shut out of any leadership roles in the abolition movement (Buechler 1990; DuBois 1978). At the Seneca Falls convention, participants drafted a Declaration of Sentiments with resolutions demanding women's rights, particularly in areas of law, marriage, employment, and the church and identifying the privileges men had over women. For example, the preamble to the Declaration of Sentiments reads, "The history of mankind is a history of repeated injuries and usurpation on the part of man toward woman, having in direct object the establishment of an absolute tyranny over her" (Papachristou 1976: 24). The Declaration also stated that man "has deprived her of the first right of a citizen, the elective franchise, thereby leaving her without representation in the halls of legislation" (Papachristou 1976: 24). While the organizers sought a range of social change goals for women, the movement came to focus on suffrage as a primary goal and, for seventy-two years, suffragists continued the struggle before they succeeded.

While the story often told of suffrage is one of white women's organizations, Black women as well as Native American, Latina, and Asian American women all worked for the right to vote. Black women, marginalized in the mainstream white women's movement, organized themselves through the Black women's club movement in groups such as the National Association of Colored Women, which had the slogan, "Lifting as We Climb." In 1920, the 19th amendment was added to the constitution, largely benefiting white women, and leaving other women still disenfranchised. For example, the Chinese Exclusion Act of 1882 prevented Chinese immigrants from becoming citizens and therefore kept Chinese women from being able to vote, even though some had worked for suffrage.[1] It wasn't until the Voting Rights Acts of 1964 and 1965 that struck down state and local barriers to voting that African American women enjoyed similar access as did white women.

In sum, the discriminatory experiences of women abolitionists led to the formation of women's rights organizations. While there was initially a range of goals addressing women's lives, suffrage became primary in the struggle as women sought to alter the social structure and the institution of government. While suffrage gave women full citizenship, it did not address inequalities among women based on race, ethnicity, and social class.

The "Doldrum Years"

After 1920, white feminists from one of the major suffrage organizations, the National Women's Party, then turned their focus to the passage of an Equal Rights Amendment (ERA), a constitutional amendment guaranteeing equal rights for the sexes (Giele 1995). The amendment reads "Equality of rights under the law shall not be denied or abridged by the United States or by any state on the account of sex" and was meant to address the way gender inequality was embedded in U.S. society, particularly government and the labor force. However, over the decades from the 1930s to the 1950s and after two world wars, women's rights, instead of gaining momentum, stalled and images of women's domestic roles dominated U.S. culture. Feminism and feminists were vilified as working against traditional and appropriate gendered roles and the mass media repeatedly told white women that they had everything they needed for a full and meaningful life, even when it did not feel that way. As a result, the white women's movement went into a state of hibernation or "doldrums" in which activists continued but in a much less visible and robust manner (Rupp and Taylor 1987). During this period, women of color continued to organize. For example, Black women continued to work in the club movement with grassroots groups that focused on racial betterment and took up a range of causes such as an anti-lynching campaign spearheaded by Ida B. Wells and others.

Midcentury resurgence

The late 1960s and early 1970s saw a reinvigoration of white women's feminism spurred by the changes in their lives that did not align with ideas of traditional white womanhood. Increased access to the labor market and higher education, mostly experienced by white women, did not come with corresponding changes in gender norms. White women were still expected to abide by the domestic roles of traditional femininity, even as their lives changed. However, women of color and poor women of all races largely did not experience the same clash of norms in their lives, having already been in the labor market and not having the same access to higher education. This difference in experience by class and race would continue to divide the movement in the coming years.

For white women, this disjuncture between gender expectations and lived experience resulted in the rise of a social phenomenon writer Betty Friedan labeled "the problem which has no name," capturing how constraining domestic roles led to unhappiness and depression (1963). Friedan was later to become the first president of the National Organization for Women (NOW), which formed in 1966 and saw women's oppression as coming from their inability to participate within institutions such as the labor force and government. NOW was formed around the ideas of liberal feminism, which saw unequal access as the main cause of women's inequality.

While it was mostly middle-aged white women who experienced the "problem with no name," younger women, such as the ones who participated in the Miss America protest, were also in a state of upheaval. Many of them were active in the movements of the New Left, which included civil rights, anti-war, and students' rights movements. Just as women had earlier in the abolition movement, as young white women worked for the rights of others, they began to see parallels with their own situations (Echols 1989; Evans 1980; Ferree and Hess 1985/95; McAdam 1988). When women tried to make these connections public they were often pushed aside. In one situation, a woman attempting to speak was patted on the head by a male organizer who said, "Move on little girl; we have more important issues to talk about here than women's liberation" (as quoted in Echols 1989: 49). While Friedan and NOW spoke to an older, more professional group of white women, the younger women of the New Left found a voice with more radicalized feminism. These women divided into two groups. On one hand, radical feminists who saw women's oppression as coming from male supremacy with gender being the primary mechanism. These were the women who saw women as enslaved to a beauty culture and protested at the Miss America pageant. On the other hand, socialist or "politicos" were women who saw oppression coming from a class system combined with capitalism which oppressed all people (Echols 1989).

While all of these groups articulated the source of equality differently, they did win some significant accomplishments, and efforts by all groups peaked between the years 1972 and 1982 with victories such as the passage of Title IX, which banned sex discrimination in publicly funded educational institutions, and the Supreme Court decision *Roe v. Wade*, which legalized abortion. Radical feminists began to organize around the issues that would later emerge with #MeToo by focusing on rape, sexual assault, and harassment and violence (Whittier 2019). This was also a time when art, music, literature, and magazines such as *Ms. Magazine* flourished, and academia began to take up critical analyses of women's lives (Taylor and Whittier 1997). Language was one such area of focus. For many feminists, a key focus was on the disparity in language around men and women. Christine Mallinson (2017) documents how feminists focused on the way "language characterizes men's perspectives and experiences as default, while subordinating those of women as separate, different, and deviant" (419). Many of the issues they found with language were with how words reinforced traditional gender norms. For example, feminists argued against honorifics for women that only allowed for "Miss" (unmarried) and "Mrs." (married). Men had the honorific of "Mr." which had no marital status attached. "Ms." was introduced as the equivalent to Mr., leading to the title of the feminist magazine, *Ms.* While feminists engaged in a variety of activism including linguistic disruption by changing spellings such as *womyn* or *herstory*, one tactic that directly attacked derogatory gender norms was to stop calling adult women "girls" as a regular course of conversation. While calling women "girls" is often seen as a compliment, feminists noted that calling adult men "boys" is universally recognized as disrespectful of their manhood. This is evident when considering how Black men have historically been called "boys" as a form of systematic subordination.

Overall, this decade was a time where many traditional gender norms for women were challenged. Women began to undo some of the norms of traditional femininity, including the assumptions that all women would become mothers, needed to marry for financial support and couldn't do "men's" jobs. As the ERA neared ratification, activists involved in all types of feminism worked together to lobby for the amendment and address opposition from anti-feminist organizations (Mansbridge 1986). Despite the amendment being ratified by 35 states, it did not meet the number needed to be added to the constitution. In 1982, the ERA was officially defeated, even though efforts continued for its ratification. (For more on the defeat of the ERA and countermovements, see Chapter 5.)

Just as we saw in the early period, this was also a time when the movement focused mostly on the lives of white women. Women of color, poor women, and lesbians struggled to be a part of the mainstream white movement. However, just as Black women organized earlier in the club movement, women of color organized separately and worked on issues around gender, race, and class (Roth 2004; Nadasen 2010). Much of this work is ignored in history taught of the women's movement, missing the important work done in what Benita Roth (2004) calls a "separate road to feminism." For example, Roth details how Chicana feminists sought a greater political presence in the Chicano rights movement and worked in organizations largely separated from white and Black feminist groups. Overall, this was a period of intense activism with critiques levied at all aspects of women's lives from expectations of beauty to institutional barriers against women. The feminism of this time examined the personal, the political, and the societal in its efforts. Yet, much of the success of this time would face a backlash as the movement moved into a more hostile environment.

Backlash in the 1980s and 1990s

While mid to late 1980s saw a downturn in the mobilization and success of the mainstream white movement, it was not the end of U.S. feminist activism. Scholars argue that throughout the history of the women's movement, it has often been declared dead or in decline each time mobilization slows. Mary Hawkesworth (2004) calls this the "premature burial" of the women's movement meant to silence activists who are challenging deeply held gender norms. Scholars also argue that the way social movements are studied can lead to movements being declared in decline. Movements that do not have a visible and robust national presence in the form of organizations and large-scale demonstrations are often seen as in decline or dead. Women's movements often embrace a range of tactics, from state-focused actions to cultural tactics, broadening the ways in which movement continuity can be viewed. For example, Mary Katzenstein (1990) argues that there has been "feminist unobtrusive mobilization" or invisible activism within mainstream institutions such as the Catholic Church and the military, where women engage in everyday resistance, working for long-term gains such as women's ordination and the recruitment and integration of women into the military. (For more on the backlash against U.S. feminism, see Chapter 5.)

Feminism in the twenty-first century

After a period of submerged, grassroots-focused feminism in the late 1990s and early 2000s, feminism and women's rights reappeared on the national scene in the form of women's marches in 2017, 2018, and 2019. The election of Donald Trump and the emergence of #MeToo (discussed in the Introduction), along with a polarized citizenry, brought women's issues back onto the streets, intertwined with the goals of other movements including #BlackLivesMatter, the environmental, trans social justice, immigrant rights, and climate change, among others. The marches addressed a variety of gender concerns, including rape and sexual assault, and issues of gender stratification such as pay equity and the glass ceiling (Reger 2019). Many of these actions such as the women's marches were the result of activism on the internet that digitally connected activists and spread the word of the demonstrations across the world. These connections can happen at an unprecedented speed, and internet-based interactions can "nourish an oppositional culture" (Crossley 2019: 72). Feminism in the twenty-first century works to adopt an intersectional perspective that acknowledges the differences between women by race, ethnicity, class, and gender expression, among other identities. Gender specific goals intertwine with other movements, infusing them with feminism. Activism continues at the community level and is spurred on by virtual activism springing up over the web, connecting activists in ways not experienced in earlier periods. However, it is important to note that divisions of race-ethnicity, social class, age, nationality, and other social identities continue to plague U.S. feminism in the twenty-first century.

Summing up

So, what does the history of the U.S. women's movement tell us about the intertwining of gender and social movements? Drawing on the idea that protest comes in cycles, we can see how the reemergence of the U.S. women's movement in the 1960s and 1970s was tied to a period of intense movement activity that included gay liberation, student, peace and anti-war, and the civil rights movements. While these explanations help us to understand the connection between different social movements, it is also clear that gender as a system of stratification embedded in society can be the impetus in the emergence of movements. Historians have examined how as society went through periods of change such as industrialization and urbanization, women's lives changed (Chafetz and Dworkin 1986), and this resulted in changes in traditional notions of femininity (Freeman 1973; Costain 1992). In sum, when society shifts in ways that reveal gender discrimination and there are resources and avenues of change available, women's movements are likely to appear or reappear.

Adding an intersectional perspective to the history of the women's movement also broadens understandings of the movement. Scholars argue that much of the story of U.S. feminism is told through the experiences of white women such as Elizabeth Cady Stanton, Gloria Steinem, and Betty Friedan. Feminist scholars, employing an intersectional perspective, document a different history. Becky Thompson (2002) argues that the often-told trajectory of the U.S. women's movement ignores how women of color were organized in separate groups and around a diverse array of interests that did not always include white women. Benita Roth concurs and documents how Black, Chicana, and white feminist groups emerged often at the same time, early in the movement. By doing so, Roth (2004) corrects the notions that organizing by women of color was always the result of the racism they experienced in white feminist groups but often they organized themselves independently and those organizations are often ignored in the "whitewashing" of feminist history. This pattern of leaving out some groups of women and focusing solely on the concerns of others is also present in movements outside the United States. For example, indigenous women in Mexico have been unwilling to identify as feminists due to the urban and middle-class nature of the movement that ignores their need to align with men for indigenous rights (Castillo 2010). Overall, when women's movements do not adopt an intersectional perspective that acknowledges differences in experiences of oppression and privilege, some women are left out. Without intersectionality, the most privileged women often become the focus of the movement.

Overall, taking a brief look at the complex history of the U.S. women's movement illustrates how shifting gender norms and gender stratification can generate social movement activism. Examining the U.S. women's movement is instructive in how gendered grievances shift over time and relate to certain groups of women. For example, the early years of the movement dealt mostly with barriers to women's ability to be independent citizens in charge of their own lives, while the later years addressed issues of access and opportunity as well as shaping what it meant to be a "woman" in society. Since social movement goals arise from gendered dynamics in society, the solutions that activists seek are shaped by their perceptions of society and women's lives. For example, the white radical feminists in the Miss America protests drew on their experiences in the New Left movements of the time and focused on how cultural ideas of womanhood were limiting and discriminatory. Their focus on social change differed greatly from socialist, Chicana, and Black feminist efforts, which were all happening at the same time. The experience of being a woman with a set of social identities such as age, class, race-ethnicity, and more in a particular society can spur a particular type of activism. This is particularly true as we examine women's movements around the world.

Women's movements exist in a variety of global contexts and often over multiple generations. However, it would be a mistake to assume that they follow the generational "wave" model seen in the U.S. movement. Indeed, "In every group, in every place, at every time, the meaning of 'feminism' is worked out in the course of being and doing" (Rupp and Taylor 1999: 382). In addition, not all women's movements are feminist. To illustrate how women's movements follow unique paths, I examine women's movements through a global lens and specifically, the case of the Chilean women's movement.

Women's Movements – Thinking Globally

Women's movements exist around the world. They often grow out of broader political struggles such as nationalist movements in South Africa and India as well as anti-authoritarian movements in Latin America (Basu 2017: 31). For example, in the case of India, the nationalist movement for independence from British colonial rule also served to give women a chance to organize and mobilize, laying the foundation for a future movement (Pal 2017). However, not all women's movements are feminist or, as in the case of Chile (see in the next sub-section), stay feminist. Myra Marx Ferree and Carol Mueller (2004) argue that there is a distinction between women as a movement's constituency – that is, the group that benefits from the outcomes – versus those who endorse a feminist identity and challenge gender inequality. Women as a constituency often emerge around a variety of gendered issues that address the rights of themselves and children, but do not seek radical change. These movements can begin with women as the group affected by the issues and, over time, become more feminist and seek to change gender norms in fundamental ways. For example, women's movements focused on citizenship and sex equity can begin with issues such as suffrage, fair and legal employment standards, and constitutional and legal rights, and develop into movements that focus on more radical transformations of gender.

Taking a global perspective illustrates how women's movements also address a range of citizenship and societal concerns such as globalization and militarism (Enloe 2007), social justice (Wilson 2007), and the labor market in the global economy (Moghadam 2005), among others. Overall, the rise of specific women's movements seen around the world is often credited to a change in women's access to resources. Social movement scholars drawing on resource mobilization and political process theories see the availability of resources, access to the politically powerful or the political system, along with work with formal organizations, as a key to the emergence of women's movements.

Transnational connections are also important to consider when thinking globally. One key example of this is the role that the United Nations world conferences on women have had on women's rights activists. Women's groups were called upon to help organize the conferences, which then brought together women's activists from around the world. This "enabled women activists from around the world to meet and collaborate, forming relationships that lasted long after the conferences ended" and served to strengthen local groups through these ties (Basu 2017: 9). As a result of the 1995 Beijing conference, a Platform of Action was created that was the "most impressive and ambitious outcome," focused on a range of issues affecting women from violence to poverty to education (Basu 2017: 10). While much of that platform was not achieved, the conferences articulated issues faced by women around the world and thus spurred the activism of community and national women's groups.

The case of the Chilean Women's Movement

Chile offers a different view from the United States as to how women's movements grow and shift over time and fluctuate from being focused on women's issues to adopting a feminist ideology. Scholar Rita Noonan (1995) identifies three basic stages of the Chilean movement. The first stage from 1913 to 1953 saw the rise and fall of feminism as the ideological foundation of the movement that focused on women's rights. During this period, women's organizations proliferated, and activists examined and critiqued women's lack of political and citizenship rights. Just as we saw in the United States, women worked for suffrage in a variety of organizations that came together, and in 1949 women won the right to vote. However, while the U.S. women's movement went into abeyance and reemerged later, the next political period in Chile was one where class concerns rose in importance over gender, and feminism was viewed as divisive and elitist. "The message [was] clear: women's strategic concerns should come after the 'real' revolution succeeds" (Noonan 1995: 91). The second phase, from 1953 to 1978, was one where women's issues were seen through the lens of motherhood or "the maternal frame." This frame saw women's involvement in politics as an extension of their roles in the family. The mother–child relationship was seen as the most important – and only – concern that women should take into any involvement in politics. Both the politically progressive and conservative forces drew on the maternal frame, effectively ending feminism and the goal of women's rights outside the family. This period saw women focus primarily on "mothers' centers" meant to address poverty. These mothers' centers proliferated and the 1960s saw an increase in maternal frame-focused community action programs and grassroots organizations.

The maternal frame held its importance in the 1970s, and in 1972 the country suffered an economic collapse that threw many into poverty and hunger. Upper-class and middle-class women protested by banging pots and pans in the streets to protest government actions (I return to this protest in Chapter 4). These demonstrations led to the development of a "feminine power" organization, *El Poder Femenino*, which engaged in subversive activities against the government. Eventually economic and hunger issues resulted in a military coup that placed dictator Augusto Pinochet as the head of government.

However, despite the repressiveness of the regime, women were able to continue their activism by aligning themselves with motherhood and family as the source of their protests. Drawing on Catholicism's traditional view of women, the Pinochet regime did not recognize wives and mothers as publicly important. As a result, women were able to take to the streets to protest the disappearance of loved ones, and consequently became the primary voice of opposition to the regime. Overall in this period, framing their activism around motherhood and family gave women access to political opportunity structures (i.e. political openings) that men did not have.

The final phase identified by Noonan (1995) goes from 1978 onward. As women worked to oppose the regime, they also became more radicalized, and feminism and the focus on women's rights outside of the family began to reemerge. As activists worked to end the hunger and poverty caused by the Pinochet regime, they added women's rights to the agenda. As such, a new ideology emerged from the protestors – the fight for the return of democracy – which did not shut out feminism, as struggles had in the past. Feminists were able to draw on the endorsement of democracy in their activism, noting how it could also apply to dynamics in the home. As a result, multiple organizations began to form, and feminist activism was visible from the 1980s onward.

Chilean feminism in the 1990s focused on building feminist spaces and media, and celebrated the election in 2006 of Michele Bachelet, the first female president (Larsson 2020). Since then, feminists have advocated for legalized abortion, non-sexist education, and the end to gender-based violence. The year 2018 saw the first women's strike, with hundreds of thousands of protestors taking to the streets. In 2019, the group *Las Tesis*, made up of four women, wrote and performed the anti-violence song *"Un Violador en tu Camino"* ("A Rapist in your Path"). The lyrics include lines such as *"The rapist is you / It's the cops / the judges / the state / the president."* The song with its choreographed movements spread through the country and the world and was incorporated into #MeToo protests when it was performed outside Harvey Weinstein's trial in New York City in 2019.

Overall, how gender issues and women are perceived has shifted in the Chilean women's movement from a feminist focus on women's rights to a maternal view of women as belonging primarily in the family and back again to feminism. The political context of the movement dramatically shaped the roles women could assume as activists with even the most oppressive regimes still having openings for women to work for social change. The current movement continues to address a range of issues with generations of women working on and identifying what needs to be addressed.

When we compare the women's movements in the United States and Chile, it is clear that the political and social context along with cultural ideas about gender can make women's movements follow different patterns and pathways. The emergence of feminism as an ideology in Chile surfaces and then is extinguished by other political forces. In the United States, we see feminism emerging and then going into abeyance with activism continuing on a subdued level. In Chile, women are still able to become activists and oppose the state through their potential as mothers and in traditional family roles. In both sites, as the culture shifts in the twenty-first century, feminism reemerges in Chile and becomes reenergized in the United States. While it is clear that the pathways of these two feminist histories are very different; there are some similarities. We can see that movements or movement ideologies can surge in certain times and retreat in others. In addition, when people are engaged in social change efforts, such as promoting mothers' centers, or in other movements, they can become radicalized, so changing the course of movements.

Whether they address women as a constituency or embrace a feminist set of beliefs, these movements, like other movements that argue for equal treatment of marginalized people, face forces and groups hostile to movement gains and to activists. While women's movements are not commonly repressed through violence, those women's movements that seek to change the status quo often face "soft repression" in the form of ridicule or dismissal of the movements' goals and tactics (Ferree 2004). This is clear in the derogatory terms about feminists that deride them for not being "womanly" enough for women or "manly" enough for men.

Women who identify as feminists have been called "lesbians" for not doing appropriate heterosexualized femininity, regardless of the individual's sexual identification, "bitches" for not being content in a subordinate position, and making unnecessary trouble or being "humorless nags," people who need to "lighten up." All these negative terms are forms of gender sanctions and have been successful at driving some away from identifying as feminists. In addition, women's movements have faced opposition from other women. These groups often argue that the goals of a women's rights or feminist movement will erode women's status in society. For instance, during the U.S. fight for the ERA, anti-ERA groups argued that the constitutional amendment would undo the special protections that women, particularly during their child-bearing years, have in the workplace. They argued that equality in the workplace, where all workers are treated the same, is not the same as equity in the workplace, where differences among groups are recognized. With the defeat of the ERA, we can see how powerful these arguments are, and that changing norms around gender is complex, with women on either side of the movement. (See Chapter 5 for more on anti-ERA activism.) Men's movements also have divisions and conflicts, which are the result of shifting gender norms.

U.S. and British Men's Movements

In a similar way to women, men have organized around concerns about masculinity and manhood, and the United States and Great Britain are two sites of these movements. Overall, men's activism around gender is complex, with activist organizations working for and against change with much of the contemporary activism taking place on the internet and social media. Masculinities scholar Michael Messner (2016) identifies two main types of men's movements: *men's rights* movements that focus on the ways in which men are aggrieved as men, and men as *pro-feminist* allies who work in groups supporting women and/or on issues such as stopping violence. Ana Jordan (2019) in her examination of men's movements in the United Kingdom sees a typology of three types of men's groups – feminists who are aligned with the women's movement, post-feminists who believe gender equality has been achieved, and anti-feminists or backlash activists who have the goal of rolling back gains of the women's movement. Men's rights groups are often a combination of post-feminist and backlash sentiment, while pro-feminist men's groups align themselves with feminism.

Messner (2016) argues that men's movements were brought on by a "historical gender formation" where the state and culture were dramatically influenced by global women's movements in the 1970s. In this period, while men experienced challenges to traditional masculinity norms, those challenges did not necessarily change men's lives in significant ways. Arlie Hochschild (1989) in her study of the domestic division of labor calls this period the "stalled revolution," in which women's roles changed dramatically but men's roles in the family did not. Overall, this was a period where accepted gender norms for women began to shift. For example, women now had more economic freedom than ever before, with more access to occupations and education, and could now do such activities as obtain credit and sign contracts without a husband's approval.

While these changes may have felt like the world was becoming more open for women, the period was followed by significant societal backlash, with aspects of men's movements playing a part (Jordan 2019). Men's rights groups were initially aligned with feminism and then diverged, becoming more anti-feminist. Pro-feminist men took a different path and largely aligned with feminists whenever possible. Both sides of the men's movement continue to be influenced by diffusion of feminism into society in the twenty-first century. Overall, as feminism and reactions to it shifted over time, so too did men's lives and their activism.

Men's rights

Messner (2016) argues that U.S. men involved in the movements of the 1960s and 1970s were inspired by the women's liberation

movement and the way in which activists engaged in consciousness raising, as well as taking on gender inequality in societal
institutions. Drawing on the women's movement, men began
to speak of their own liberation, first adapting feminist claims
of sexism to their own lives and addressing how sexism could
both privilege and harm men. By the 1980s, men's rights groups
began to shift and moved from aligning themselves with women's
liberation. Instead, they argued that male privilege was a myth
and men were just as harmed by sexism as women. Books such
as Warren Farrell's 1974 *The liberated man* and Herb Goldberg's
1976 *The hazards of being male* represented these views. The
key to these arguments is how men and women are equally hurt
by patriarchy, and the rejection of the idea that men always
oppressed women.

As the women's movement experienced a backlash in the 1980s
and the 1990s, the men's rights movement also shifted. Along
with the cultural change brought by the women's movement, the
1980s and 1990s were a period where changes in the economy
and labor force eroded some of the opportunities experienced
by mostly poor and blue-collar men. Messner (2016) notes that
some have labeled this period "the decline of men." Experienced
globally, this is a period where unemployment, the decline of
labor unions, economic restructuring, and the rise of neolib-
eralist thinking meant that less privileged men had fewer and
fewer resources and opportunities. This resulted in a period where
young working-class men faced challenges to their gender identities as income earners and providers for the family (Connell
1995). By the 2000s, the result was a society concerned with the
"war against boys" and the "decline of men." This concern still
resonates globally. For example, Isabel Pike (2020) documents a
concern with the neglected "boy child" in Kenyan society, which
results from the perception that the media focuses too much on
girls' and women's inequality. Pike traces the idea that men have
been disempowered by women's rights to the rise of the idea of
man as breadwinner for the family. She notes that British colonial
rule disrupted traditional gender relations, establishing the man
as the "head" of the family and setting in place gender relations

more common in the West. As Kenyan women have mobilized for equality, it is often perceived as coming at a cost to men's rights and masculinity.

In the United States, as a result of this shift away from feminism, men's rights groups are less likely to attack feminist gains such as Title IX directly but are more likely to hold anti-feminist ideas (Messner 2016). The career of men's rights activist and writer Warren Farrell follows this trajectory. Connell (1995) notes that Farrell was initially aligned with the more liberal type of feminism and critiqued the "masculine value system" which gave men privilege. However, by the 1980s, Farrell argued that too much attention had been paid to women and more scrutiny was needed of men's situations and women's forms of power. In one of his later books, *The myth of male power*, he writes:

Professional women – powerful women – often have the most difficulty understanding male powerlessness. Why? Powerful women tend to connect with powerful men. Less powerful men like their garbagemen – are invisible to her. And what she sees of the powerful man is deceptive: Powerful men are best at repressing their fears.

A professional woman is more likely to know the name of her secretary than her garbageman. And therefore more likely to know how her secretary experiences men than how her garbageman experiences women. Because a less powerful woman tends to work in the office and a less powerful man tends to work outside the office (e.g. in hazardous jobs), she is more conscious of the dilemmas of the less powerful women around whom she works. The powerful woman doesn't feel the effect of the secretary's mini-skirt power, cleavage power, and flirtation power. Men do. The powerful woman tends to use these forms of power much more cautiously in the workplace because she has other forms of power. Taken together all of this blinds the professional woman to the powerlessness of the great majority of men – who are not at the tip of the pyramid, but at its base. And without the sexual power of many of the females at its base. Nor does she feel, via her hormones, the vulnerability of the man at the top to a woman who wants him – why the desire for sex, affection, excitement, and the desire to be desired would lead President Clinton to risk his entire future and his past [referring to his affair with Monica Lewinsky]. (1993: 21–22)

Farrell maintains that he is not an opponent of the gains brought by feminism, but he notes that a movement is still needed that allows men to speak about their experiences (1993: 20). Similar arguments state that some masculine norms and activities, such as engaging in prostitution or pornography, facing rape accusations, or charges of domestic violence, are not evidence of men's privileged status but instead are instances of men as victims.

The population of men drawn to rights groups are largely white and privileged (Heath 2003) with much of the contemporary ideology spread through websites. Current anti-feminist/men's rights groups include organizations such as the National Coalition for Men (NCFM) whose website includes the statement, "Since 1977, NCFM has been committed to ending harmful discrimination and stereotypes against boys, men, their families, and the women who love them" and includes a slide show on feminism as a hate group (NCFM 2020: online). Other groups include religiously oriented groups such as the Promise Keepers, a Christian group that draws on a traditional interpretation of the Bible, stating their goal is to "mobilize men and their families to be the generational catalyst for our culture today" (Promise Keepers 2020: online). In common with all of these groups is the belief that women's rights and, feminism in particular, have created an ideology that misinterprets how gender inequality functions in society.

Pro-feminist

Pro-feminist groups did not see patriarchy in the same manner and noted that even with narrow conceptions of what a "true man" is, men still benefit from adopting norms of masculinity. What made the pro-feminist or as Connell calls it the "radical wing of Men's liberation" different from men's rights is a "focus on contesting the social inequalities of gender, especially the subordination of women" (1995: 220). Organizations addressing men's privilege emerged internationally, evident in Europe, Australia, and the United States. In the 1980s and 1990s, organizations such as the National Organization for Men against Sexism (NOMAS) in the United States and campaigns such as the White

Ribbon Campaign in Canada emerged. NOMAS describes itself as a "pro-feminist, LGBTQ+ affirmative, anti-racist" organization "enhancing men's lives" (NOMAS 2019: online). The White Ribbon Campaign commemorates the fourteen women gunned downed in an anti-feminist attack at the University of Montreal in 1989. The campaign notes that "since 1991 men have worn white ribbons as a *pledge to never commit, condone, or remain silent about violence against women and girls*" (White Ribbon Campaign 2020: online [emphasis in the original]).

The White Ribbon Campaign also exists in the United Kingdom and was started in 2007 with the goal of ending male violence against women. Jordan notes that the group has the additional goal of allowing "men to redefine traditional ways of working together via their activism in WRC, promoting unity rather than the competition characterizing most male-dominated organizations" (2019: 135).

Other men, drawing on decades of feminist activism, continue to work as allies to women, particularly in anti-violence work (Messner et al. 2015). Scholars Kelsey Kretschmer and Kristen Barber (2016) note that even in the 1970s, when anti-violence campaigns such as Take Back the Night March were women-only, men found ways to be allies, working on the sidelines or serving as support staff. By the 2000s, some of the most visible pro-feminist activism was around anti-violence organizing, often focused on violence toward men, by men. However, Messner notes that the identity "pro-feminist" does not resonate with men working on anti-violence activism. "Today's men who are engaged in anti-violence work spend less time agonizing over labels – in fact, the younger of these men are often disinclined to label themselves at all" (Messner et al. 2015: 17). Men who are anti-violence allies often become professional activists who find their careers through a melding of feminist ideology and anti-violence work.

While much of what men's rights activists and anti-violence allies address are norms around masculinity, some men draw on femininity in their activism. For example, the "Walk a Mile in Her Shoes" march, which started in California and spread across the globe, is one such event where men participate in an annual

"Walk a Mile in Her Shoes" event in downtown Fayetteville, NC.
Credit: Lewis Perkins/Paraglide via Fort Bragg/Flickr

one-mile walk wearing four-inch, red patent leather high-heel shoes. Scholar Tristan Bridges, who studied five such marches, notes that the overall goal is to make men aware of the issues and get them involved in anti-violence activism. He notes that the event presumes that wearing high heels will make for a *"novel* and *transformative* experience" for men (2010: 14 [emphasis in the original]). The organizers of the march are often women who work for non-profit groups that serve victims of violence and use the march to raise awareness through a positive (and fun) lens.

"Walk a Mile in Her Shoes" illustrates the complexity of gender and social movements. "Walk a Mile" endorses a symbol of traditional femininity – the high heel – to make feminist-inspired change. Yet, some feminists view the high heel as a cultural symbol representing women's inequality. High heels are critiqued as impeding women's ability to move while emphasizing their bodies as sexual objects for the male gaze. Indeed, the radical feminists highlighted at the opening of this chapter included high heels as one of the "instruments of torture to women" tossed in the "freedom trash can" (Echols 1989: 93). "In fact, high heels are part of the systems of inequality that help to ensure that it will be *women* who are assaulted and abused" (Bridges 2010: 15 [emphasis in the original]). While the marches have positive benefits such as raising awareness and money for non-profit and addressing violence, the overall message of the marches is somewhat conflicted. Bridges concludes:

> "Walk a Mile" marches unintentionally reinforced the taken-for-granted view that femininity and masculinity *and* homosexuality and heterosexuality are completely different and opposed. Beyond that, the marches implicitly identify concerns with violence against women as "feminine," thereby continuing a historical tradition of gendering feminist politics. (2010: 21–22 [emphasis in original])

Jordan makes a similar argument in her analysis of "Heels Walks," organized by the UK White Ribbon Campaign. She notes:

> WRC [White Ribbon Campaign] Heels Walks could be seen as transgressive of gender norms as men perform a (limited) femininity in the context of promoting an explicitly feminist message. However, the humour surrounding the walks is clearly in the deliberate feminization/emasculation of the men. (2019: 143)

Therefore, even when activists seem to move beyond traditional gender norms (i.e. men in high-heel shoes), gender norms are not necessarily challenged. Indeed, actions that seem to challenge the gender binary, such as women in men's suits or men in "feminine" shoes, only serve to reinforce the sense that there is a core difference between men and women, thereby reinforcing the binary (Lorber 1994). The academic focus on "Walk a Mile" marches illustrates how gender scholars add to the study of social movements as well as learn from them.

Studying masculinity

Just as feminist scholars turned their attention to gender and femininity, masculinity, in part prompted by men's activism, also came under scrutiny. Pioneering scholar Raewyn Connell argued that men's privileges and perspective of the world have been shaped by the gender identity of hegemonic masculinity (1987, 1995). Hegemonic masculinity is the form of dominant masculinity that is most valued by a culture and society during a particular time (Connell 1987, 1995). A cultural ideal, hegemonic masculinity is a gender identity that legitimates patriarchy and other forms of inequality and can vary in form at different times and in different societies and cultures. In the United States and other Western countries, hegemonic masculinity is often manifested as heterosexual, white, young, and physically fit. Indeed, Connell notes that there are historical and global variations that are the "currently accepted" strategy of promoting men's dominance set in particular place and time (1995: 77).

Because hegemonic masculinity depends on the subordination and dominance of the "other" (i.e. women, gay men, non-white men, other lesser valued masculinities) as its core, one of the major challenges it faces is feminism. While it is tempting to assume that men open to feminist ideas do not embrace a hegemonic masculinity when it comes to gender identity, scholars Tristan Bridges and C. J. Pascoe argue that even forms of masculinity that look more open to gender equality retain aspects of dominance. Pascoe and Bridges call this "hybrid masculinity" to capture how men may do masculinity in ways that seem non-conforming but that still align with hegemonic masculinity (2014, 2018). As such, men can retain their relative positions or authority and power. Men who do hybrid masculinity may take on identities that seem oppositional to traditional masculinity, or combine characteristics such as acting "feminine," "soft," "gay," or metrosexual among other practices. Bridges notes that hybrid masculinity could be called "hybrid hegemonic masculinity" because of the way it retains privilege through "discursive distancing," which situates other groups of men as the "real problem" (2021: 664). This form of more "feminine" and hegemonic masculinity is evident in the "Walk a Mile in Her Shoes" marches. Events seeking to address issues of gender inequality, such as anti-violence efforts, can also embrace aspects of gender inequality in the form of high heels.

Other variations of hegemonic and hybrid masculinity can also be found in anti-feminist men's groups. Melanie Heath, in her study of the Promise Keepers, argues that the group in the 1990s sought to change the norms of masculinity. They urged men to be more caring and attentive to women and children, while at the same time encouraging men to take a firm leadership role as head of the family. Heath draws the analogy of masculinity to an egg and labels Promise Keepers' masculinity "soft boiled" in contrast to the more "hard-boiled" hegemonic masculinity (Heath 2003: 423).

Men's Movements – Thinking Globally and Intersectionally

Because men's movements often arise in conjunction with women's movements, they also exist across the world. However, where women's movements, as evident in the case of the United States and Chile, can follow different paths, men's movements often follow the patterns evident in the United States and Great Britain, particularly in groups focused on ending gender-based violence. For example in South Africa, the rape trial of a high-profile government leader drew responses from what scholar Elaine Salo calls the "critical men's movement." Organizations such as *Sonke* Gender Justice Network and Men as Partners Network spoke out, articulating how "militaristic [and] ethnonationalist meanings of masculinity" were a part of the trial (2010: 46). Indeed, men around the world have organized in anti-violence movements focusing on rape, sexual assault, and/or domestic violence (Flood 2005). In addition to international campaigns such as the White Ribbon Campaign, there are anti-violence organizations formed by men in India, Nicaragua, Namibia, Malawi, Kenya, Zimbabwe, and Australia. These movements often draw on a range of tactics to educate men and stop gender-based violence such as educational films, guerilla theater in bars, pamphlets, and walks (similar to the "Walk a Mile" campaigns) (Flood 2005).

Just as pro-feminist movements are evident around the world, so are anti-feminist or men's rights movements. Masculism as countermovement to feminism is evident in Canada, and Poland is the site of a men's rights movement that aligns with anti-feminist organizations (Leek and Gerke 2020). Fathers' rights organizations are evident in the United States as well as Canada, Australia, Denmark, Sweden, Norway, Iceland, and Finland. These are "political groups formed to focus on men as fathers and that demand a stronger influence of fathers in the lives of their children – particularly after divorce; they allege that family law favors mothers and victimizes fathers" (Leek and Gerke 2020: 453). Overall, Western societies are a strong influence on men's anti-violence movements globally. Along with an international lens, an intersectional perspective is also essential to understand men's movements.

Adopting an intersectional lens on men's activism from the "Walk a Mile" participants to the Promise Keepers, we can see how gender intersects with other social identities such as race and sexual identity. For example, Bridges found that as a white man he was able to march unnoticed and study the other male participants in a "Walk a Mile" march (2010). In addition, he found that marchers often drew on homophobia to establish their heterosexuality. Men who walked too competently in the heels were seen as transgressive (e.g. deviant) versus men who tottered on their heels, struggling to walk. Bridges traces this to stereotypes about gay men and drag performances. Heath found that the mostly white men in Promise Keepers embraced discourses of gender and racial equality but did little to address institutional sexism and racism. Instead, the organization encouraged men to focus on personal and spiritual solutions to sexism and racism. Intersectionality allows us to see how Promise Keepers and anti-violence activists function as *men* in movements as well as heterosexuals and whites in social movements. By broadening the view of gender to include other social identities, intersectionality allows a more complete and nuanced view, moving us past thinking just about men or women in movements. Indeed, it was the concept of the "universal woman" in the women's movements that spurred the theorizing by Black feminists, who argued that not all women fare the same in society and led to the current use of intersectionality in movements and scholarship.

In sum, like women's movements, men's movements are organized around gendered grievances and shaped by the societies around them. For men's rights activists, the core gender issues are ones of masculinity and its costs through a largely anti-feminist lens. These activists often view these costs as equivalent to those that women bear living under a patriarchal system. Pro-feminist men align their gender concerns with feminist ideologies and find that patriarchy is harmful to women in ways it is not to men. A key concern in pro-feminist organizing is to fight violence in all forms, particularly against women and children but also considering violence against men, by men.

Conclusion

The 1968 Miss America protest at the beginning of this chapter was one made up of young, white radical women who sought to change how the gendered expectations of being a "woman" shaped their lives. While this protest was captured (mostly negatively) in the U.S. imagination, it was just one aspect of a complex movement. This protest illustrates the complexity of movements structured around single-gender concerns in multiple ways. First, single-gender movements tend to "universalize" one group, often the most privileged, and marginalize others. The development of intersectionality and the adopting of an intersectional perspective can reveal the complexity of people's lives and therefore, movements. Second, single-gender movements are made up of groups who often take a multitude of approaches in their work for social change. The history of the U.S. women's movement illustrates this dynamic with all of its divisions, coalitions, surges, and periods of low activity. Third, the pattern of activism in movements varies by context as the case of the Chilean women's movement illustrates, and often movements are entangled and influence each other as seen in the men's rights and pro-feminist movements. Finally, single-gender activism can spread into academic research and bring new understandings to the study of gender as we have seen in the development of concepts such as hegemonic and hybrid masculinity.

Overall, taking a look at how women and men have organized around gender concerns illustrates one way that gender is relevant in social movements. This chapter addresses how gendered people organize around issues related to the norms, expectations, and limitations they collectively experience in their lives. This leads to the question – what is the relevance of gender in mixed-gender movements that are not specifically organized around gender inequality? How does gender shape these movements? It is these questions that I turn to in the next chapter.

Sources to Explore

Suffrage Movement (U.S. and Global): From the National Women's History Museum. https://www.womenshistory.org/resources/general/womans-suffrage-movement

From Britannica online. https://www.britannica.com/topic/woman-suffrage

Equal Rights Amendment: From the Alice Paul Institute. https://www.equalrightsamendment.org/history

Global Women's Movements: Amrita Basu (ed.) 2010. *Women's movements in the global era: The power of local feminisms.* Boulder, CO: Westview Press.

From UN Women. https://www.unwomen.org/en/what-we-do/leadership-and-political-participation/womens-movements and https://interactive.unwomen.org/multimedia/timeline/womenunite/en/index.html#/

Walk a Mile in Her Shoes. The official website https://www.walkamileinhershoes.org/

Questions to Consider

1. How are women's movements shaped by the political and social context around them? Compare the history of the U.S. women's movement to the Chilean women's movement.
2. Draw on the Miss America protest to explain why feminists have been marginalized and stereotyped in society. How would a social movement scholar explain this?
3. How do grievances differ between the women's movement and the men's rights movement? How do they differ between the men's rights movement and the pro-feminists? What does this tell us about gender norms and reactions to them?
4. What does the concept of hybrid masculinity do to our understandings of contemporary masculinity? How is it evident in the example of the "Walk a Mile in Her Shoes" protests?
5. What does an intersectional perspective add to our understanding of gender and social movements? Where does this perspective originate from?
6. Contrast the view of men in the men's rights and the pro-feminist groups. How does adding an intersectional perspective and considering race and social class address these views?

Reflection

We have seen that many of the divisions that occur in social movements, such as the women's and men's movement, happen because people have different views on how gender shapes their lives. Can you recall a time when your gendered worldview differed from that of those around you?

2

Gender in Movements: What Happens in Multi-Gender Movements

Volunteer college students sing "We Shall Overcome" as they prepare for their journey as part of the Freedom Summer 1964 campaign.
Credit: Ted Polumbaum/Newseum collection

As a white college student in the northern United States, you come to hear a speaker discussing the civil unrest happening in the south. It is 1963 and the speaker, an organizer from a Black student activist group, tells stories of Black citizens and activists being beaten, intimidated, and

55

murdered for attempting to register or recruiting people to register to vote. The speaker ends the lecture with a plea for your help. If you are willing (and brave enough), they will train you on how to do community organizing in the very communities where the violence and unrest is occurring. You (a young white woman) decide to sign up along with your best friend, a woman you have known since your first days on campus. You are both interviewed by the white, male, community organizers and asked how fast you can type and if you want to work to help set up a community center. You are disappointed by the options, since you are pre-law and wanted to focus on voter registration. Afterwards you talk to one of your male friends. You find out that his interview was quite different. He was asked about his willingness to go door to door, facing danger from hostile whites, and if he was prepared to go to jail for his actions. You decide to go but your friend backs out. Her parents won't support her during the summer saying it is too dangerous. When you get to Mississippi, you find that you spend a lot of your time doing clerical work in the office while your male friend is out in the community, doing the more valued face-to face interaction of trying to register local residents to vote.

While parts of this scenario may be reminiscent of activism around voter disenfranchisement in the United States today, it is actually based on a book by social movement scholar Doug McAdam. In *Freedom Summer* (1988), McAdam sought out the volunteers from the 1964 campaign by the same name that had the goal of registering voters in Mississippi. At this time, only 6.7 percent of registered voters in the entire state were Black due to a system of institutional barriers combined with a campaign of terror and intimidation.[2] This was so pervasive that in some Mississippi counties with a majority of Black residents there were no registered Black voters. This, along with the grinding poverty and lack of educational opportunities, led McAdam to describe Mississippi as "the living embodiment of the potential for inhumanity and injustice inherent in the [U.S.] system" (1988: 24). In some parts of Mississippi, Black residents who attempted to register to vote were asked to read a section of the Mississippi state constitution and interpret it, often having to do so for an illiterate white county clerk. Even attempting to register could bring violence and intimidation to residents, such as a cross burning on the front lawn or being threatened at gunpoint.

Organized by Student Non-Violent Coordinating Committee (SNCC), civil rights activists sought to change this culture and system of voter disenfranchisement through the Freedom Summer campaign. However, SNCC had faced multiple failures in their efforts to register Black voters in Mississippi. To address this pernicious system of structural racism, SNCC decided to use white privilege as a way to make change. They purposely sought out white, elite college students for the campaign, with the goal of engaging the students' privileged parents and their networks, as well as drawing media attention. As a result of their recruitment, more than 1,000 people joined the campaign working in 44 local projects over the summer. Overall, the Freedom Summer campaign was largely made up of white students from elite colleges and universities, who were funneled into different jobs based on their sex. These jobs were largely gendered. Men did the more "daring" work of voter registration and community organizing, whereas women often found themselves doing more of the organizational and domestic work, such as clerical duty or teaching children in Freedom schools.

The gender dynamics of Freedom Summer serve as an excellent introduction to the ways in which gender as a process and structure sorts how people experience multi-gender social movements. McAdam found that not only did women and men do different work in the Freedom Summer campaign, they also faced different expectations and barriers (1992). Despite their higher rates of previous civil rights activism and organizational affiliations, women had lower rates of acceptance into the summer campaign. McAdam, in part, attributes this to different gender stereotypes, with men being viewed as more fearless, intrepid and willing to take risks, and women needing protection and being better at detail-oriented tasks or those that involved nurturing. He also notes that in the recruitment process women applicants were evaluated for their appearance and physicality, criteria not applied to men. Once on the project, women also faced issues around sexual politics. In addition to facing sexual harassment, women found themselves constrained by the sexual double standard where men's sexuality was not questioned but theirs was under scrutiny. For instance, one woman was judged as acting in a way "not becoming a project member" and had to leave the project (1992: 1224). This double standard also had a racial component. "If a white woman accepted a Black man's sexual advance, she risked being ridiculed as loose; if she spurned him, she left herself vulnerable to the charge of racism" (Echols 1989: 30). Many of the white women volunteers would come to view these experiences, particularly with the white male organizers, through the lens of sexism, identifying them as objectifying and exploitative (Evans 1980).

While it is tempting to believe that the gender inequality experienced in Freedom Summer is long past, contemporary movements still struggle with gendered assumptions of roles and abilities. In the Occupy Wall Street protests starting in 2011 (discussed in more detail in Chapter 4), the treatment of women and gender queer leaders varied greatly from men (Hurwitz 2019). Gendered assumptions also played a role in the 2020 Black Lives Matter protests with the "Wall of Moms" protected by the "Wall of Dads" (discussed in more detail below) (Blum 2020). Looking to the past and at the present, gender continues to be a factor in how people experience movements.

Drawing on the lessons from Freedom Summer as well as other movements, in this chapter, I examine how men and women can fare very differently from each other in the same movement. In Chapter 1, I examined movements organized around a single gender and related issues; however, often movements do not have a specific or obvious connection to gender. Kevin Neuhouser (1995) calls these "gender generic movements," ones that integrate both men and women for goals that appear less gendered, such as voter registration or lobbying for the passage of a law. Yet, social movement participants bring with them their gendered understandings of the world and act on gendered assumptions, expectations, and beliefs. These beliefs can establish a hierarchy in movements in which masculinity and manliness is prized over femininity and womanliness. Examples of this gender stratification system include valuing high-risk activism, such as violent confrontations and risking death, over everyday or more submerged activism, such as organizing community groups or participating in support groups. Verta Taylor (1999) notes that this gendered hierarchy of activism can shape all aspects of social movements, including how they mobilize, lead, and strategize with participants, as well as adopt ideologies and achieve outcomes. To begin to explore these dynamics, I first examine how women and ideas of femininity and womanhood are incorporated into social movements. Drawing on social movement research, I focus on two prevalent themes: women *not* being seen as activists or being viewed through the lens of motherhood. I then explore the research on men and movements, focusing on how masculinity and manhood is often made invisible in social movements and when it is visible, men are seen through the lens of "warriors" and risk takers.

Womanhood, Femininity, and Movements

Many of the analyses of how women are treated in these kinds of gender generic movements come from activists themselves. A key example is the 1965 manifesto by Casey Hayden and Mary King, white civil rights activists. Hayden and King, both veteran activists who had worked with SNCC, circulated a memo among other women activists, asking for a dialogue about the inequality women faced in society, as well as in the movement. Inspired by the analysis of racial discrimination, in their essay "Sex and Caste: A Kind of Memo," they note that in their work for civil rights, they had come to see how women are also oppressed (1965). They noted that male activists usually responded with laughter and ridicule to their conclusions, spurring the departure of women from male-dominated organizations. Their realization of the gendered nature of power was key in the reemergence of the U.S. women's movement in the 1960s and 1970s. Hayden and King's memo illustrates the gender dynamics of multi-gender movements, which include not being seen as legitimate activists and only being viewed through a gendered lens. To examine how women fare in movements not specifically focused on gender issues, I first begin with how they have been left out of characterizations of "the activist."

Women aren't "real activists"

Judy Taylor in her study of Irish feminism succinctly notes, "When feminists organize, they are often treated first as women, then as activists" (1998: 686). This assumption that women cannot, and should not, be activists derives from past cultural ideas that society is divided into a public sphere to be ruled by men, and a private sphere that is the domain of women in the home. This divide also has a racial component, with, historically, white women active in the public sphere – work, government, education – seen as anomalies and deviants. This led to the idea that "political participation is perceived to be normal for men. In contrast, women's participation has been seen as anomalous, ineffective, and sometimes inappropriate because it contradicts gender expectations" (Einwohner et al. 2000: 681). This assumption is evident in Freedom Summer where ideas of appropriate gendered behavior played a substantial role in the recruitment for the campaign. In a review of the applicants for the project, McAdam (1992) found that women applicants were much less likely to participate in the Mississippi campaign. The reasons for this ranged from family concerns for their daughters and the potential danger to women to recruits balking at the mostly domestic and clerical work assignments. Exacerbating this problem were the recruitment interviewers' narrow views on how women could be involved. However, it is not just organizers' biases that keep women from being viewed as activists. Scholar Karen Beckwith (1996) argues that it is also the attention paid to women by the media. In her study of British coal mine closures, she notes that when women are involved in movements that focus on men's lives and work – in her case, coal miners – women activists were either completely ignored or only individual women were singled out for attention, leaving the impression that there was no collective effort by women.

As noted, these ideas of women belonging more to the private than the public have long roots in history. Taking a look back on the labor strikes during the Gilded Age in the United States (1870–1900) expands Beckwith's more contemporary conclusion that women engaged in collective action are often not taken seriously. In a study of 2,930 strikes from 1881 to 1886, researchers found that the more women who were involved, the less likely the strike's chance of success (Jacobs and Isaac 2019). This can be attributed to negative attitudes toward women in society, held both by males on the picket line and their male employers. At this time, although now entering into the labor market in increasing numbers, women were mostly concentrated in a few industries and were viewed as incompetent and dependent on men, therefore deserving lower wages. Media coverage of women strikers often noted they "flirted" more than demonstrated and were "out of control" and immoral (2019: 755).

Returning to the issues raised by Hayden and King, it was not just white women who found themselves marginalized within movements. Black women in the late 1970s grew frustrated with both the civil rights and the women's movements, according to scholars Aisha Upton and Joyce Bell (2017). Black women activists were marginalized by racism in women's movement organizations, which prioritized white women's lives and aspirations as a goal. They were also frustrated by the lack of opportunities to be activists due to sexism in the civil rights movement, which viewed men's ambitions as the most important in the movement. However, although unacknowledged, Black women's activism in communities was effective and aided the movement. For example, Freedom Summer afforded Black women volunteer opportunities in leading and directing their own locally focused programs, although they remained less prominent in the public roles of national leadership (Evans 1980). The result of this community work along with marginalization in movements was the radicalization of Black feminism and the articulation of intersectionality and the experience of multiple oppressions (Upton and Bell 2017).

In addition to sex and race, women's sexual identity has also been a barrier for their participation in movements, and consequently, their visibility as activists. There is a history of women's exclusion from activism in LGBTQ+ movements, as well as the U.S. women's movement. Lesbians in early U.S. LGBTQ+ movements, then called the homophile movement, often formed their own organizations rather than work in the mostly white male groups. This was due to how men used personal networks to recruit, and male public and commercial space, such as bars and restaurants, to meet, serving to segregate men and women (Rupp, Taylor, and Roth 2017). In the resurgence of the women's movement in the late 1960s, lesbians struggled to participate, finding that their presence and concerns in groups such as NOW were not welcomed. Betty Friedan, then president of NOW, infamously labeled lesbians the "Lavender Menace" fearing that they detracted from the group's ability to achieve their goals.

In sum, ideas of womanhood, femininity intertwined with racial and sexual identities, often stood in direct opposition to the image of the activist, who was often conceived of as a white, heterosexual male who was daring and risk-taking with leadership potential. Despite these stereotypes, women *do* participate in social movements. Indeed, Lee Ann Banaszak and Holly McCammon (2018) argue that scholars are beginning to document how women have played important roles in a range of movements from the far right to environmental, civil rights, and nonviolent movements, among others. And it is often a gendered identity that drew them there and shaped their protests.

Women as gendered activists

My husband spent thirty face-years as an underground union coal miner. My father was a coal miner, my grandfather was a coal miner. I have brothers that are coal miners. Living in southern West Virginia, you of course grow up around coal. My husband was a very, very proud coal miner. I believe that coal mining has been an honorable profession; I just believe that the time for coal has come and gone. As I become more aware of the damage that fossil fuels are doing to the climate, and as I think of the generations to come – what will be left for them? I feel a really desperate need to try and do something to change it.

Lorelei Scarboro quoted in Bell (2013: 121)

In her book, *Our roots run deep as Ironweed*, Shannon Elizabeth Bell draws on the stories of white Appalachian women engaged in the fight for environmental justice. Scarboro, quoted above, engaged in multiple forms of community activism including fighting against mountaintop-removal mining which has a devastating effect on the environment, causing multiple health issues for the nearby communities. Bell documents the stories of Appalachian women to capture their importance in the environmental movements. She argues that although women make up a substantial amount of the membership and leadership in grassroots activism, they have not been acknowledged. Indeed, she notes how important women have been in fighting a range of environmental concerns, often centered on the communities they live in. This activism, she argues, emerges from a "protector identity" that extends from women's gendered identities as mother and nurturer.

Activist Helen Caldicott echoes this idea. Reflecting on her work in the anti-nuclear movement, Caldicott said, "Women have a very important role to play in the world today . . . using their positive animus to save the children of the country and the world . . . The [anima] must become the guiding moral principle in world politics (as quoted in Marullo 1989: 4). This focus on "saving the children" and the world is evident in a range of movements. Focusing on the anti-nuclear movement, scholar Sam Marullo (1989, 1991) found that women thought about activism differently from men in the Greater Cleveland Nuclear Freeze Campaign. Women were more likely to believe in the symbolic and more expressive and interpersonal goal of the movement than men, who focused more on the instrumental, goal-oriented actions. In addition, many more women were drawn to the campaign, making up approximately 65 percent of the membership.

Women also have a long history in peace and anti-war movements with women-only events such as the 1915 Women's Peace Parade held in the United States. This focus on peace and anti-war movements can be seen around the world with women's protests in Chechnya, Chile, Japan, Indonesia, Sudan, and Pakistan. Although not always recognized for their efforts in these movements, women are seen as more collaborative than men and more adept at finding solutions (Hunt and Posa 2001).

As we will see, these gendered ideas around women's activism, such as caring for children and being more collaborative, are influenced by the process of gender (as in gendered identities), the intertwining of structure and gender (seen in organizations and networks) as well as gender stratification (evident in the roles and perception of women in movements). I first start with a discussion of motherhood as a core organizing identity for women in movements.

What Shannon Bell is addressing in her concept of the "protector" in her discussion of white Appalachian women is an expansion of how scholars have conceptualized much of women's activism through gendered socialization and expectations. That is, motherhood (or expectations of motherhood) can profoundly shape women's engagement in social movements. Using the identity of a "mother" as a lens, a significant amount of women's activism is seen as shaped by the idea that caring for community is an extension of caring for family. Scholar Carol Mueller (1987) calls this the development of gender consciousness; in this instance, the gender role of motherhood means caring for community. This gender consciousness then shapes the boundaries and reasons for engaging in a social movement. Much of the research on women and movements illustrates how – while the activism in gender generic movements (i.e. movements not focused on addressing gender inequality) is done by both men and women – it is the gendered identity of women as mother, nurturer, and protector of generations that can draw women into participation. Indeed, women activists often say their reasons for engaging include making a better world for their children, protecting their daughter's future rights, or serving as "mothers" of all humankind.

Once in a movement, women can use domestic roles to maintain, support, and expand it. For instance, Kathy Blee (2003), in her study of women in the organized racism movement, also referred to as white supremacy, found that women were expected to care for the "collective family" and to help create a sense of camaraderie for the group. This sense of family was about more than building solidarity in the individual racist groups but that "modern organized racism is based partly on familial expectations and ideologies, however distorted" (2003: 124). Motherhood and issues around motherhood are also used to promote action within other social movements, particularly feminism. For example, Verta Taylor (1999) found that women in the United States who had experienced postpartum issues worked in a self-help movement to change notions of motherhood, policies, and medical practices. She argues that these issues are more than problems of the individual but are the result of gender stratification.

Understandings of motherhood in social movements could also vary. In my study of two NOW chapters, I found that motherhood was interpreted in two ways: as a social status needing attention and as a personal experience. The New York City chapter of NOW viewed motherhood as a marginalized and gendered social status requiring feminist attention and one of the chapter's many social issues. In the Cleveland NOW chapter, motherhood was also seen as a personal experience that drew women into activism. Many of the Cleveland women discussed how it was the personal experience of motherhood that compelled them to become activists. (Reger 2001).

Motherhood is also an identity that can link women together in networks, and these networks can be mobilized to draw women into activism. This is called micromobilization, the process by which people are drawn into movements due to their interactions with others. Overall, it is not only the identity of mother or nurturer that can draw women into social movements, but also how gender identities (such as mother) connect women into networks, organizations, or communities. These places serve as spaces for mobilization into movements. As evidenced in Bell's Appalachian women, it was gendered informal and community-based networks that drew women into environmental community-based activism. These networks and their politicized gender consciousness are then reinforced through interaction. For example, Verta Taylor (1996) finds that postpartum support groups, which appear to be apolitical, can, in fact, be politicized spaces. These often sex-segregated networks are fertile spaces for movement recruitment (1996: 169).

However, as we can see in the case of Freedom Summer, this gendered identity of women as primarily motivated by caring for others can be problematic in movements. McAdam found that many of the young women volunteers resisted the pull to become "mothering" activists and sought the more exciting and dangerous work the men were doing (1988, 1992). Returning to the case of the Chilean women's movement in Chapter 1, it is also clear that seeing women as activists only through the lens of motherhood can limit their potential for making significant changes to gender inequality. Noonan argues that the adoption of motherhood as the source of women's activism, also "mirrored the dominant discourse espoused by the authoritarian regime of Pinochet" (1995: 91). In another study of Chile, Jacqueline Adams (2002) examined what happens when a movement of women activists declines in a strongly patriarchal society. As the movement slowed, she found that women activists often returned to the traditionally gendered work and duties expected of them and did not explore new gender norms. In sum, motherhood might be a significant ideology bringing women into activism, but it can also limit attempts to change gender inequality.

In addition, doing the gendered work of caring for others kept some women from seeing their actions as activism. Jenny Irons (1998) tells the story of Aurelia Young, a Black woman who did not see her care work as a form of civil rights activism in the U.S. even though others clearly did. Irons reports, "When Freedom Riders came to Mississippi in May 1961, Young housed those students who were arrested as they came out of jail, and she served as a 'conduit' for taking items donated by people in the community to students in jail, supplementing their diets with orange juice and vitamins. She also fed civil rights workers and attorneys in her home; although she worked as a music teacher at Jackson State University, her kitchen was known as one that never shut down" (1998: 699). Irons concludes that Young's work fits with the description of activism, and the civil rights movement would not have been successful without women like her and their work.

It should also be evident from the examples from Freedom Summer and Appalachian environmental campaigns that how women experience motherhood and activism varies by race-ethnicity, class, religion, ability, and other social categories. Nancy Naples (1992, 1998) in her study of African American and Latina women community workers coined the concept of "activist mothering" to explain how women are pulled into activism that extends their personal, family, and community experiences. The concept of activist mothering captures the ways in which gender, race, and class can draw women into particular types of activism. For example, the women who joined Mothers Against Police Brutality (MAPB) did so as mothers whose children had been killed by the police, but also as women who sought to push back against the marginalization of their Black and Brown children. Scholars Anna Chatillon and Beth Schneider (2018) argue that MAPB members work against more than the occurrence of police violence, but also the devaluation of Black and Brown mothering in the United States. Summarizing the literature on Black motherhood, they argue that in a society rife with stereotypes, "... Black mothering is criminalized through the carceral system and infringed upon by social and child welfare programs" (2018: 247). MAPB activists contest this marginalization by describing their children's deaths and emphasizing the lack of an official response. In addition, these activists continue to view themselves as engaged mothers, even after the death of their children, and work to change police policies. Overall, Chatillon and Schneider argue that the group does more than draw on motherhood but "draws on activist mothering's entwining of parenting and politics, response to discrimination, and connection to broader racial and ethnic community organizing" (2018: 253).

Activist mothering can be seen in a variety of movements including fighting police brutality, rejecting plans to place toxic waste in neighborhoods, and working for immigrant rights. For example, the idea of "family as a political subject" worked to draw Latinas into the immigrant rights movement in Chicago, changing the script from negative anti-immigrant images to ones of family and togetherness (Pallares 2015). Mary Pardo (1998) documents the formation of the group Mothers of East Los Angeles (MELA), by women primarily of Mexican origin, in the 1980s. The goal of

MELA was initially to stop a state prison planned in the women's neighborhood. The group later took on rejecting the placement of a toxic waste incinerator in the community. Successful in both of these campaigns, MELA continued to work on issues and in the 1990s split with groups dividing up to work on a range of issues including water conservation, job generation, community investment, lead poisoning, immunization awareness, graffiti removal, and college scholarships (Pardo 1998).

Applying an intersectional perspective to gender and social movements is not limited to only considering race-ethnicity. Kayla Stover and Sherry Cable (2017) find that in their examination of women involved in the environmental movement, class is an important social identity. They argue that working-class women from all racial and ethnic groups often initiate and lead environmental justice movements. This is evident in the anti-toxic waste movement and the anti-environmental racism movement.

Overall, despite women's struggle to be seen as activists in movements, women have participated in meaningful ways. Often those ways are spurred by their roles as mothers and protectors of their families and communities. While the identity of mother or potential mother can be a strong influence in drawing women into social movements, it can also limit their activism. The identity of mother is also one that varies by race-ethnicity, class, age, and culture among others and mothers from different social locations come to movements shaped by a constellation of experiences. I next examine how men have been studied in multi-gender movements.

Manhood, Masculinity, and Movements

Whereas women are viewed first through their gender identities and then as activists in movement, men are often characterized as activists with little scrutiny as to how gender shapes their activism. When men are seen through a gendered lens, it is often as "warriors" who do high-risk, dangerous activism, ignoring other forms of activism in which men can engage. When men are seen as gendered, it is often the result of an intersectional perspective. I start this discussion of masculinity and manhood with a focus on how gender is often ignored in examining men's activism.

"Invisible" masculinity in movements

While scholars have turned to women's gender socialization and a focus on motherhood and caring in order to understand their participation in movements, men's gender socialization is often less scrutinized. Historically, scholars have identified men's activism as just activism and ignored how, it too, is gendered. This originates from a conception of activism as a gender-neutral activity with men expected to be key players (Pardo 1998). Doug McAdam (1988), when reviewing social movement research, notes that gender is one of the most important factors mediating social life, but research on individual activism has paid little attention to it. Indeed, the very conception of "an activist" is often conceptualized as a man. As a result, women are often viewed through the lens of gender, whereas men are often seen as *just* activists.

Returning to the example of Freedom Summer, we can see how women were confined to more feminine roles in the campaign, such as clerical work and teaching, and men to the more dangerous work of canvassing neighborhoods. Although gendered divisions of labor in movements may seem sensible in getting the work done, there is more than practicality in these divisions. Raewyn Connell reminds us that "'masculinity' does not exist except in contrast to 'femininity'" (2016: 31). In other words, what women do in movements is often understood as the opposite of what men do, and what men do is simply "activism." In her study of masculinities, Connell (1995) identifies different types; the risk-taking "live fast and die young" man, the pro-feminist "new world" man, "a very straight gay," that is, gay men who strategically and self-consciously negotiate with heterosexuality, and the expertise-driven "men of reason." While we have seen how pro-feminist men have been a part of the men's movement, it is the risk-taking "live fast" masculinity that is often captured in social movement studies, and is often seen as the opposite of the "nurturing mother" identity of women in movements.

Indeed, the expression of masculinity in movements can come at the cost of acknowledging women's efforts. Judy Taylor (1998) documents how men can co-opt women's movements and labels this dynamic "friendly fire." Friendly fire comes when gender dynamics within a movement shut out involvement by those who do a less masculine style of participation. She sees this in ways in which women's attempts to organize are ignored, belittled, directed, or co-opted, and argues that "friendly fire" needs to be negotiated for women to effect larger change. Jody Chan and Joe Curnow (2017) document some of the ways in which men do "friendly fire" in a multi-gender social movement through what they call "exclusive talk" and doing "expertise" in meetings. Exclusive talk is when two or more people focus their conversation on each other, despite others present in the meeting. They argue that this "had the effect of relegating women and people of color to the sidelines during many important decision-making conversations and implied that the White men who participated in exclusive talk were more knowledgeable and experienced" (2017: 81). Doing "expertise" is established when white men in the group dismiss ideas from white women and people of color and focus on pursuing bureaucratic and administrative avenues. Exclusive talk and doing expertise are two examples of not acknowledging the dynamics of masculinity, with the result of making masculinity and masculine norms "invisible" in movements. Karen Beckwith (1996) in her study of women's efforts to keep coal mines open in the United Kingdom sees a similar dynamic. She observed that men were seen as the most legitimate actors and women were only able to establish their credibility through their family statuses, like mother or daughter, and their roles as working-class women in the community. However, unlike femininity, when masculinity is visible, it is often not as a family role but instead as a "warrior" for social justice.

Men as warriors

1968 in Boston, Massachusetts – the Vietnam War is raging and young men are being selected for the draft. Anti-war activists use a variety of tactics to protest the war with a focus on stopping the draft. One group, the New England Resistance, reaches out to men by emphasizing risk-taking actions such as burning their draft cards and risking jail. One member says, "Here us straight middle-class guys from the suburbs are getting ready to go to prison, to become felons, to wear uniforms and be known by a number, it surprises people." Another man, when noting how people respond to their non-compliance [with the draft], said "It really blows their minds ..."

"Protest and the problems of credibility"
Barrie Thorne (1975)

In the late 1960s, sociologist Barrie Thorne studied the anti-war movement to investigate some men's strategies for avoiding the draft for the Vietnam War. Although she was not initially focused on gender, she observed that women in the movement "often found themselves in a marginal and ambiguous position," relegated to introducing the organization, the New England Resistance, to out-siders and fielding encounters that were often perceived as having sexual overtones (1975: 114). As such women were peripheral to the group, men were the core, and recruitment of men drew on masculine norms. Key in their recruitment was the promotion of risky behavior to prove one's masculinity, fitting with Connell's characterization of the "live fast and die young," risk-taking man, as well as men's activism in Freedom Summer and the anti-nuclear movement. McAdam (1988) notes that for the men, participating in Freedom Summer "could be seen as functionally equivalent to any number of other traditional challenges that were available to young men as part of the process of 'becoming a man,' 'seeing the world,' or 'testing one's mettle'" (1988: 57). Men in the anti-nuclear movement also embraced aspects of the warrior activist. In a survey of attitudes toward nuclear weapons, men were more likely to believe that a nuclear war was controllable and nuclear weapons serve some purpose (Marullo 1989, 1991). Researcher Sam Marullo argues that these beliefs are consistent with tra-ditional gender socialization. "Traditionally men have been in control of the use of force and are more likely to see it as a tool ... Furthermore, to the extent that the male role continues to be more macho oriented, more readily relying on force and hiding on fears, even the more peace-loving men in the freeze movement show less fear of the Russians and less fear of nuclear war" (1989: 19).

This idea that "true" activism and masculinity are connected can also be found in movements across the political spectrum. Kathy Blee observed that "Stereotypical traits of masculinity, especially physical strength and aggression, are presented as both the prerequisite and the consequence of white racist activism" (2003: 113). In a contemporary example, after the election of Joe Biden in 2020, groups for and against Donald Trump clashed in a series of interactions in which large numbers of men participated. One pro-Trump group, The Proud Boys, purposively sought out anti-Trump and Black Lives Matter protests, throwing firecrackers, burning signs, and clashing with other protestors and the police. Proud Boys, a group with ties to white nationalism, have been described as a "male-chauvinist organization" who "roamed the streets looking for a fight" (Hermann, Lang, and Williams 2020: online). Groups like the Proud Boys can be seen as a part of an "alt-right"" movement in the United States and parts of Europe. Scholars Cliff Leek and Marcus Gerke (2020) see this as a movement that is "intensely gender[ed]" without being about gender. They note:

> The alt-right is a heavily male-dominated social movement that includes many antifeminist elements but gender politics are rarely the explicit driving force behind their organizing. Yet, ideas about the supremacy of white and Western men and constructions of (white) women as in need of protection from men of color (e.g. African Americans or Muslims) often feature prominently in alt-right thought. (2020: 457)

While the Proud Boys draw on masculinity in their white nationalist identity, there also exists a widespread community on the internet that embraces the "warrior" identity in the battle against feminism and women. Leek and Gerke (2020) observe:

> In a loose transnational network of online communities, websites, blogs, social media accounts, and message boards, often referred to as the "manosphere," antifeminist ideas are discussed, and political

action as well as online harassment of perceived political opponents (women, feminists, progressives) is planned and carried out. (454)

They note that some act in the community "in openly misogynistic ways – sometimes to the point of advocating violence against women – and explicitly embracing men's claim to superiority" (455). Included in the manosphere are groups such as PickUpArtists, Incels (Involuntary Celibates), and Men Going their Own Way (MGTOW), which are active on message boards and online forums such as reddit and 4chan.

While the notion of physical and aggressive masculinity can pull men into movements, stereotypes about men and the connection to high-risk work, can keep men from activism. Shannon Bell and Yvonne Braun (2010) find that men are outnumbered by women in environmental justice activism because of the connection between masculinity, risk, and work. They argue that men see working in the coal industry as a type of job fitting with a hegemonic masculinity that deters movement involvement. Women's identity as both "mothers" and "Appalachians," (e.g. regional citizens) allows them easier access to activism. In other words, "real men" work in the mines, not against them. It is important to note that where women are often seen as mothers in a movement, rarely are men seen as fathers. It is more common for men to be called the "father" (founder) of a movement, than it is to see their role as parents as key in activism. Because of this, when men draw on the gendered identity of father in protest, it gains attention. One striking example of this in Black Lives Matter protests (discussed more in Chapter 3), men lined up in front of other protestors as a "Wall of Dads" who came out to protect against the violence aimed at the "Wall of Moms" and other protestors.

When risk and a masculine identity are linked in social movements, it is a powerful combination. McAdam (1986) defines high-risk activism as having some sort of "anticipated danger" and does not credit either men or women as more likely to engage in it. However, the model he describes that leads an individual into engaging in high-risk activism has gendered components. He begins with family socialization being a factor, whether or not someone will engage in a social movement. Yet, we know that gender socialization varies for boys and girls and cannot be assumed to be the same in all cases. McAdam then notes that contact with other activists brings a participant into low-risk/low-cost activism (such as signing a petition). To go from low-risk activism to high-risk activism, he argues that a key component is biographical availability, defined "as the absence of personal constraints that may increase the costs and risks of movement participation, such as full-time employment, marriage, and family responsibilities" (1986: 70). He goes on to write:

> The costs and risks of protest activity are not equal for everyone. Suppose, to the earlier description of our hypothetical college student I add the information that he is neither married nor employed. Clearly the costs and risks he must weigh before entering into more intense forms of activism are much less than they would be for, say, a full-time custodial employee of a nuclear plant with a family of five to support. The extent and number of such constraints further condition the availability of a person for high-risk/cost activism. (1986: 70)

While the concept of biographical availability is useful to the study of social movements, it is necessary to include gender and how women's and men's socialization, expectations, and lives may differ as to who is available. Adding to those differences can be religion and culture. For example, to explain how some Muslim men are socialized to engage in martyrdom for Islam, Frank Hairgrove and Douglas McCleod (2008) look at the role of small religious study circles. They argue that young men are socialized to combine masculinity and religious teachings into their world view, allowing them to engage in "high risk activism," and often fatal action, without a concern for self.

While the concept of the "masculine warrior activist" has been identified in some movements, overall masculinity and activism is underexplored. Rachel Einwohner and her colleagues argue that masculinity needs more attention and propose a more complex view:

> Although it has received far less analytic attention from scholars of gender, masculinity is similarly multifaceted. Men are variously rep-

74

resented in the United States, for example, as fathers, warriors, and rational decision-makers. These general stereotypes, like those of women, are further subdivided. Warriors can be conceptualized either as aggressors and perpetrators of atrocities or as protectors of women, children, and nations. As with femininity, however, these images are finite and are focused around certain culturally resonant stereotypes. (2000: 683)

Despite a significant lack of attention to masculinity in social movements, men's other social identities, such as race-ethnicity, and sexual identity, have been the focus of studies. Men are often recruited as both men and members of another social category. For example, Blee finds that white ethnic masculinity is essential in organized modern racism. As such, a core part of recruitment into organized racism is the idea that white men are losing their "rightful" economic, social, and political privileges. She argues that "Aryan masculinity is venerated as the bedrock of the white race, racist politics as the litmus test of masculine prowess. Assumptions

The 1968 Memphis Sanitation Workers' Strike.
Credit: Bettman / Getty Images

about masculinity are crucial, as the methods used by racist movements to appeal to white men make clear" (2003: 112). This intertwining of masculinity and race is evident in other movements and movement campaigns.

Whereas in the case of organized racism, where white men fight to maintain their privileges, men with marginalized racial-ethnic identities fight to obtain their rights. Key to the civil rights movement was the sense that Black men (and women) deserved dignity along with equality. In the civil rights movement, the 1968 strike by sanitation workers is an example of the intersection of social class, race, and masculinity. Sanitation workers in Memphis worked in unsafe conditions for extremely low wages (approximately $1 an hour). Their strikes did not garner much community support until two workers were killed in an equipment malfunction. Their deaths brought the support of local ministers with Dr. Martin Luther King Jr. coming to town to speak at a rally. The sanitation workers, all men, asserted their right to safe working conditions and decent wages by carrying signs reading, "I Am A Man." In doing so, they claimed their right for dignity as Black men doing work, highlighting the intersection of race and class with gender. Memphis State University students also understood this connection between masculinity, race, and dignity, shown by their carrying signs at an earlier march that read, "Decency is due every man" and "Dignity for all" (Honey 2007). This call to be seen as men has its origins in racist stereotypes in which Black men were often called "boys" by whites, no matter what their age. Sanitation worker Taylor Rogers explained the slogan, saying, "'I Am A Man' meant freedom. All we wanted was some decent working conditions, and a decent salary. An[d] to be treated like men, not like boys" (as quoted in Honey 2007: 211). Historian Michael Honey (2007) reminds us that "Throughout most of American history, and especially for workers and the racially oppressed, exercising one's 'manhood' meant standing up for one's rights to freedom and full citizenship. By using the first-person pronoun 'I,' the sanitation workers constructed themselves as the authors of their own liberation" (212).

Freedom Summer was also a place where race and masculinity

intersected. Many Black male volunteers were interested in, and had, relationships with white women during the summer campaign (Echols 1989; Evans 1980). These relationships were prompted, in part, by a history that prohibited any interaction between the two, and violence and murder for Black men even suspected of approaching white women. Historian Alice Echols writes, "Of course, the interracial relationships that developed in these projects often grew out of genuine caring and affection. But some black men used white women in an effort to reclaim their manhood and some white women used black men to prove their liberalism ..." (1989: 30). These relationships were common throughout the summer and caused rifts between white and Black women and were discouraged by some of the organizers.

Masculinity also intertwines with other social identities in movements. Many contemporary LGBTQ+ organizations have roots in the 1950s homophile movement, which was largely made up of white men (Rupp, Taylor, and Roth 2017). At this time, men and women did not share many of the same issues. The focus of the movement in the early years was largely on the police entrapment of men for cruising and engaging in public sex, issues that were largely not shared with women at the time. The Mattachine Society was one of the first organizations formed in the United States around the issues of homosexual oppression. Founded by Harry Hay in 1950, the group eventually came to argue that the heterosexual family was the foundation for individuals' understanding of themselves in terms of gender. Traditional gender norms (i.e. "father" and "husband" joined with "mother" and "wife") did not provide any role model or gender guidance for homosexuals. This lack of a visible gendered alternative to heterosexuality, they argued, created homosexuals as an "oppressed cultural minority" (D'Emilo 1998: 65). While the initial analysis of the gendered nature of heterosexuality appeared to draw lesbians into the movement, early organizing stayed focused on men and masculinity. "In numerous, often unconscious ways, male homosexuality defined gayness in terms that negated the experience of lesbians and conspired to keep them out of the Mattachine Society" (D'Emilo 1998: 92–93). While later organizations were to become more integrated, the early years of the LGBTQ+ movement illustrate how the lens of sexual identity intersected with masculinity and shaped the movement.

Other identities intersecting with masculinity include those men who have come forward as victims of sexual assault, rape, and bullying. By doing so they reveal some of the ways in which stereotypes about the invulnerability of men do not make them immune to victimization. Nancy Whittier (2009) in her study of child sexual abuse notes how for men, it is important to identify visibly as survivors. She quotes one man as saying:

> The message I have told men is . . . it's your duty as a survivor to give a voice to these issues and the reason it is your duty is because [you should] think of yourself as that child. What you needed then was to hear men come forward and speak openly with courage and without shame about sexual victimization, the same message women get . . . (2009: 179)

Here the call is for men to acknowledge that an abuse often thought of as only happening to women, should be made visible as an issue facing boys and men. Indeed, Whittier notes that the most common cases that resulted in imprisonment were between a female victim and a male offender. While this fact confirms that most victims are females, it also works to solidify the stereotype that men are immune to sexual abuse. Relatedly, Messner and his co-authors note that men who come to anti-violence activism often do so after working through their experiences of not having "measured up" to conventional masculinity (2015: 147).

Overall, masculinity has been somewhat invisible in social movements and not examined to the extent femininity has. Men have been conceived as risk-taking warriors both in and outside movements. A clearer picture of how men function in mixed sex movements emerges when an intersectional lens is applied, revealing how men organized to maintain privilege or fight for their rights as men of a certain race, ethnicity, class, or sexual identity. When men fail to achieve all the privileges of white, invulnerable, heterosexual masculinity, those marginalized identities intertwined with gender can bring them into social movements. The difference between fighting to retain rights and fighting to achieve rights is the result of a hierarchy of masculinity that is at the core of a society.

Societal Concerns and Shifting Gender Norms

While many of the types of gendered activism can come from rather static stereotypes (i.e. men as warriors and women as mothers), shifting gender concerns in society can also shape movements. Carrie Baker (2018) in her study of the U.S. youth sex-trade movement documents how concerns about children and adolescence in the sex trade corresponded with periods of expanding women's rights as well as times of increased anxiety about youth and sexual behavior. Baker examines how a range of concerns including economic changes, immigration, and xenophobia, as well as shifts in the lives and opportunities for women and children, brought anxiety about "naive white girls" being tricked or ensnared into prostitution by foreign men or men of color. The movement to protect these girls drew on gendered notions and a "crisis of 'girls at risk' discourse" (2018: 222). The result was a distinguishing of victims, with cisgender girls more likely to need protection and rescue but cisgender boys more capable of taking care of themselves. Baker notes that this hierarchy of victims was also racialized, with girls of color seen as needing less protection because of stereotypes about their presumed lack of innocence.

Baker makes several relevant points in her examination of gender in a multi-gender movement. First, conceptions of gender, age, and race (to name a few) are not static and shift as societies move into different economic, political and social periods of time. Second, these shifts can become the foundation for rationales in movements, bringing new narratives to who is and isn't a victim worthy of societal concern. In Baker's study, white girls became the focus of concern with boys and girls of color less so. Social movements are organized around ideas of inequality and oppression. If a group is not recognized as victims, regardless of their grievances, no movement will be organized around them. Fortunately, we live in a world that acknowledges that boys, girls of color, trans girls and trans boys are victims of sexual abuse and are pulled into the sex trade the same as cisgender white girls. Yet, anti-violence and anti-trafficking activists continue to argue that we still do not pay sufficient attention to those who are not cisgender, female and white.

Conclusion

This chapter starts with the Freedom Summer campaign and how organizers assign jobs and duties by sex. Women took on the more feminized work of typing, cleaning and teaching while men took on the more masculinized (and dangerous) work of canvassing communities and registering people to vote. While this division of labor is clearly gendered, Freedom Summer also offers other lessons on how gender shapes multi-gender movements. First, historically gender has shaped who is thought to be an activist and what they are capable of achieving. Women, through gendered roles such as mother, often pass unnoticed as activists (as the case of Pinochet's Chile documents.) Men, on the other hand, are seen often as the "default" activists and can have their gender and sex remain invisible in accounts of social movements. Yet, despite the ungendered characterization of men's activism, masculinity is a key in men's participation in movements. While women may not be pulled into movements to prove their "womanhood," men are often pulled into movements to prove, assert or protect their masculinity.

Second, while gender is a component in how activists do activism, we have multiple examples of other important, intersecting factors. For example, race and sexuality shaped activists' experiences very differently in the civil rights movement. Region and class continue to shape the environmental movement in Appalachia. Sexual identity intertwined with sex and gender shape experiences in the LGBTQ+ movement. An intersectional perspective adds dimension to our understanding of gender in multi-gender movements, moving us beyond one-sided portrayals of activists.

Taking all these dimensions into consideration, it is still clear that gender sorts and organizes how people fare and experience social movements. In Chapters 3 and 4 we will examine how this sorting shapes how movements bring people into movement and the very path that movements can take.

Sources to Explore

1964 Freedom Summer campaign. https://www.history.com/topics/black-history/freedom-summer

1968 "I Am A Man" protest. https://www.civilrightsmuseum.org/i-am-a-man

1984–1985 Lancashire Women's campaign against mine closures. https://www.wcml.org.uk/our-collections/protest-politics-and-campaigning-for-change/lancashire-women-against-pit-closures/

Questions to Consider

1. How did gender shape how men and women activists experienced the Freedom Summer campaign? Can you relate this shaping of experience to other areas of life?
2. How is motherhood or the notion of motherhood important to social movements? What are some positives of this connection? What are some negatives?
3. How is the characterization of "the activist" gendered? How does this influence our view of history and social movements?
4. How does the 1968 sanitation workers' strike express an intersectional perspective with the slogan "I Am A Man"? Why was this slogan so important to the campaign?

Reflection

In a mixed-sex setting in your life, are men and women treated the same? Have you ever seen a woman experience "friendly fire" as defined by Judy Taylor in the Irish feminist movement? Can you see gender norms and expectations at play here?

3

Coming to the Movement: How Gender Influences Pathways to Activism

Protestors march in Minneapolis the day after the killing of George Floyd.
Credit: Stephen Maturen/Getty Images

It is May 25, 2020. As a pandemic of Covid 19 rages across the nation, people find their lives drastically altered. In many cities and towns, restaurants, grocery stores, gyms, and daycare centers – among other business – impose restrictions, limiting or shutting down their services. A sizable segment of the country begins to work at home, communicating online and drawing on social media as a way of interacting in the world. In Minneapolis, police stop George Floyd on the suspicion of using a counterfeit $20 bill. Police officer Derek Chauvin handcuffs and pins Floyd to the ground and kneels on his neck for 8 minutes and 46 seconds, suffocating him. The interaction is filmed on a cell phone and almost immediately goes viral. Outraged Minneapolis citizens stream into the streets chanting "Black Lives Matter" and Floyd's last words, "I can't breathe." Feeding the protests are other fatal encounters with the police – some from the past such as Breonna Taylor, Eric Garner, and Michael Brown. Over the spring and summer, the country erupts in protests with sister marches held across the world. Most are peaceful but there is rioting and destruction of property in some cases. As the spring moves into summer, the interactions between protestors and the police grow more intense. One such place is Portland, Oregon, a predominately white city, that holds the country's attention as the daily interactions between the police and protestors grows more and more violent with each passing day. On June 6, 2020, more than a half of million people across the nation came out to protest, leading the *New York Times* to call Black Lives Matter the largest social movement in history (Buchanan et al. 2020).

In 2012, Trayvon Martin, an unarmed teen, was fatally shot by George Zimmerman on a neighborhood watch. Zimmerman was eventually acquitted of murder but not before the case garnered national attention, resulting in protests held in several cities. Three women – Alicia Garza, Patrisse Khan-Cullors, and Opal Tometi – tweeted out the hashtag #BlackLivesMatter, creating what was to become a social movement organization focused on ending police brutality and systemic racism. By the fall of 2020, Black Lives Matter Global Network Foundation Inc. with forty chapters had been created and the hashtag was known through the world. Active throughout the 2010s, Black Lives Matter's mission is "to eradicate white supremacy and build local power to intervene in violence inflicted on Black communities by the state and vigilantes" (Black Lives Matter 2020: online).

The presence of Black Lives Matter throughout the 2010s illustrates how movements and movement organizations get people to engage in protests and to continue to believe in, advocate, and work for the movement goals. Social movement scholars call this process one of recruitment – or joining up – and mobilization – becoming active. In this chapter, I focus on how movements connect to people through networks, how they convince people to join and then move people into becoming activists. These steps are the pathways to activism and are shaped and influenced by gender. In Chapters 1 and 2, I covered how people live gendered lives and are shaped by constraints, oppression, and expectations resulting from the gender binary. In this chapter, I explore a core concern of social movement scholars – how gender is present in the processes and pathways that bring people into social movements. While Black Lives Matter may seem to be a gender generic movement with a mixture of activists, gender plays a role in the ways people come to movement, the messages that draw them there and the activist identities they adopt. I start by examining how people's social locations play a role in coming to movements and then explore how movements reach out to potential participants. I end the chapter by discussing how emotions are gendered and play a role in making activists.

Recruitment

Simply stated, the invitation to join in activism or a movement is the process of recruitment. Yet, *how* people are recruited is not as simple. Social movement scholars view recruitment as occurring for a mixture of reasons, including the articulation of a problem/grievance by the movement, the overall opportunity or availability of a person, and people's surrounding networks. Chapter 1 focuses on how gendered grievances, along with resources and political opportunities, can result in gender-specific movements. For example, women's movements focus on the ways in which women's lives are constrained and oppressed by social norms and how shifts in society open pathways for their emergence. Also examined is how the gendered focus of one movement can inspire another movement to emerge in the example of the men's movement in the United States and Great Britain. Yet knowing about these movements and agreeing with their ideas does not necessarily mean you will join them. People need to have time in their lives to participate. In addition, the people around them can also increase (or decrease) their chances of joining a movement. These two factors, personal availability and networks, are also shaped by gender. I first discuss how pathways to movement participation can be gendered, drawing on Black Lives Matter and other social movements as examples.

Personal availability

Personal availability is the result of having space and time in one's life to participate in a movement, along with a lack of commitments or barriers. Scholars label the lack of actual or perceived personal barriers "structural availability" (Passy and Guigni 2001) and openness in one's life to participation "biographical availability" (McAdam 1986: 70). When we consider how in the spring of 2020 people were largely confined to their homes with other avenues of social interaction cut off, the role of personal availability in Black Lives Matter protests is evident. Whereas at other times, people might have still found the video of George Floyd's death infuriating and upsetting, other everyday time commitments such as set work hours, travel time to and from work, and family commitments, could have become a barrier to participation. So, for some protestors, more time to use social media, the decrease of commitments outside the home, and the fact that the protests were outside (one area seen as safer to gather in), the pandemic set the scene for more personal availability to engage in protests.

However, the removal or diminishing of barriers is not enough to encourage participation, people have also to have the ability to manage other expectations in their lives. Social movement leaders often look for participants who have few other commitments and more time, resources, and support to get involved. For example, intensive campaigns that need sustained activism may seek people, often the young, or those without formal employment, who may have fewer family or financial obligations. Freedom Summer, profiled in Chapter 2, is such a case. Organizers sought young adults enrolled in universities, who had less barriers to participation, and most likely had no occupations and diminished or no family responsibilities. This openness is called biographical availability with these students having an "absence of personal constraints that may increase the costs and risks of movement participation, such as full-time employment, marriage, and family responsibilities" (McAdam 1986: 70).

Biographical availability is gendered, particularly in societies where women and men have different roles in marriage, family, and the workforce. Those who identify as women may experience restrictions to social movement activism by their combined roles of mother, wife, daughter, and paid worker. While the status of mother may encourage women to become activists, the time commitment and other barriers may keep them from it. Scholars Kraig Beyerlein and John R. Hipp found that in the United States, "Presumably because of gendered norms of the West, marriage poses particularly significant costs and risks of activism for women, and thus decreases their willingness to protest" (2006: 315). Gender dynamics in the home can also play a role in family dynamics. Sherry Cable (1992) found that women not in the labor force were more likely to join an anti-tannery campaign run by the Kentucky Yellow Creek Concerned Citizens (YCCC). Essential to their involvement was men's willingness to engage in household labor, increasing the amount of time they could donate to the campaign.

If we consider how gender shapes life opportunities, it is clear that gender can influence the perception of whether or not you can engage in activism. That perception can be colored by gender norms and the risk of being held accountable for deviating from them. Looking back in history, an example of a perceived barrier comes from the campaign for suffrage in the United States. The media openly attacked suffragists and their platform. The *Syracuse Daily Star* published this derogatory "apology" in 1852 for covering the movement illustrating how potential suffragists would be viewed:

Our usual amount of editorial matter is again crowded out this morning by the extreme quantity of gabble the Women's Righters got off yesterday. Perhaps we owe an apology for having given publicity to the mass of corruption, heresies, ridiculous nonsense, and reeking vulgarities which these bad women have vomited forth for these past three days. (Papachristou, 1976: 44)

While newspaper coverage like this did not physically prevent women from becoming a part of the movement, the perception that they would be viewed negatively – that is, stigma – by their families, friends, and neighbors is a perceived structural constraint. These barriers to protest exist across the world. For example, in Zimbabwe women were discouraged from identifying as feminists, as the political environment became more hostile to women's activism (Essof 2010). In another example, in 1990s Poland, feminism was "so pejoratively loaded that for a long time it was considered political suicide for a woman active in public life to identify herself with feminism and feminist issues" (Matynia 2010: 203).

In addition, the type of activism expected can also serve as a barrier. Low-risk activism is often easier than high-risk activism for people with multiple personal barriers. People often weigh the costs of participating before they join. For example, for people engaged in Black Lives Matter protests, as the summer of 2020 progressed and the interactions between protestors and the police became more heated and violent, their involvement shifted from low risk to higher risk. This might have kept some from participating in later demonstrations. Gender also can play a role in that assessment of risk and those with caregiver duties might choose lower risk activities. According to scholars Kraig Beyerlein and Kelly Bergstrand, "... while signing petitions does not involve significant time away from work or children, participating in protest events does, and because this activity could result in arrest, there is potentially an additional risk for those who are employed or who are primary caregivers of children" (2013: online). So, as we can see in the 2020 Black Lives Matter protests, when barriers such as time commitments are low and risks are low, people may have more opportunities to participate in movements. This is particularly true for women who are primary caregivers and may seek low-risk ways to participate in movements.

Gender intertwined with social class can add more barriers to participation. For instance, while young working-class women and men in college may not be married or have children to keep them from joining a movement; they may need to work to support themselves in school or their families, experiencing more financial barriers to participation. Gender combined with age can keep girls from being seen as "real" activists. They may face more opposition from their parents than boys do for joining protests and can face sexism in the organizations they join (Taft 2010). For example, consider the case of young environmental activist Greta Thunberg. Thunberg was criticized as being too angry, the pawn of her parents, and as mentally ill by a host of public commentators, including in tweets from Donald Trump. Overall, gender is a factor in personal availability; however, examining gender with other social identities allows for new insights as to who gets involved with social movements and who does not. So, when people have few barriers to engaging in social protest, what promotes their activism? The answer lies partly in networks that connect people to each other and consequently can connect them to a movement.

Gendered networks

Scholar Jo Freeman (1975) argues that if people are not linked together in a meaningful way a movement cannot emerge. Once a network of potential activists is connected to a movement, the goal is to mobilize them. Mobilization is the process of making participants involved and active in the movement. As discussed in Chapter 2, often the networks that people belong to are gendered. This can be around a gendered family role and identity such as mother or father. Mothers are often connected through a variety of networks which makes for convenient "chains" of similar women who can be reached by social movement.

Networks perform three basic functions for social movements. They connect potential participants, educate them on the issues being protested, and shape their decision to become involved (Passy and Giugni 2001). Networks can also vary in form. They can be networks among groups that exist before a social movement emerges. Freeman (1973, 1975) in her study of the U.S. women's movement argued that pre-existing communication networks – those that are able to share information among individuals and organizations – were key in the resurgence of feminism in the 1960s and 1970s. Indeed, Freeman argued that interlocking communication networks are key to the emergence of all social movements where "information, ideas, contacts, and some resources were shared" (1975: 231). In the case of the U.S. women's movement, the networks were not only gendered, that is, made up of like-minded women, but also were shaped by their ages and political education. Older women were more likely to be connected through formal organizations such as state and federal Commissions on the Status of Women. Freeman argues that these women were more likely to draw on traditional forms of activism such as lobbying and petitions. Younger women "inherited the loose, flexible, person-oriented attitude of the youth and student movements" and were connected through small, informal groups that embraced more radical forms of activism such as consciousness raising groups and street theater (1973: 797).

While feminism of the 1960s and 1970s depended on face-to-face interaction, the example of Black Lives Matter at the start of the chapter brings a more contemporary focus to networks. As in the case of #MeToo in the book's introduction, social media was the site of the networks that connected individuals who may have little or no face-to-face interaction. However, even social media draws on pre-existing networks. Two of the women who founded Black Lives Matter, Garza and Cullors, had been friends for several years and were connected through Facebook (Finn 2020). This social media connection between Garza and Cullors formed an informal network that existed outside of an organized group. These informal networks are often embedded in communities (real and virtual) where people know each other. In the case of Garza and Cullors, they became Facebook friends after attending the same conference (Finn 2020).

Indeed, the more people you know in a social network who are activists, the more likely you are to become active yourself (Snow et al. 1980). Informal networks can also be gendered and differ between men and women. Women are often embedded in more social and friendship networks than men. This is due, in part, to male socialization. A range of factors, including homophobia and connecting intimacy with other men to homosexuality, can limit men's intimate networks (Nardi 1992). Informal networks can include kin networks where individuals come to know and experience social movements and then work to connect other family members. These connections can be intergenerational. For example, in a study I did of young feminists in the United States, I found that young women from the Midwest often took the lessons from their Women's Studies classes back to their mothers, prodding them to adopt a more positive view of feminism and, at times, engage in feminist activism (Reger 2012). In another example, scholar Rita Stephan (2019) documents how Lebanese women activists use extended family networks (*"mahsoubieh"*) in their activism. She finds that even within patriarchal structures of a traditional family and religion, women use these kinship connections to advocate for women's equal citizenship rights. She writes:

> They [Lebanese women of different statuses] establish their credibility in society through their family name and the position it occupies and are influenced by it. They use the family name as a passcode that creates access, credibility, and recognition as they engage in activism that ever so slowly chips away at the overt power of the patriarchal system of dominance. (2019: 623)

Intersectionality offers an even more complex view of networks. In her study of white and Black women in the civil rights movement, Jenny Irons (1998) found that grassroots and community religious networks drew Black women into a movement, spurred on by their personal experiences of oppression. Irons relates how activist Unita Blackwell, project director of SNCC (Student Non-Violent Coordinating Committee), first connected to the movement when speakers came to her church. However, Irons found that white women were more likely to become active through national organizations that were more formally organized. For example, activist

Jane Schutt, through her work with the group Church Women United, was asked to participate in the first Mississippi advisory committee of the U.S. Commission on Civil Rights. Here we can see how race and gender shape the networks women belong to and how those networks are organized differently and have different consequences for participation. In addition, an intersectional view can illustrate how networks can offer opportunities for activism that overcome some of the barriers people experience. Scholar Aldon Morris (1984) argues that the Black church was a needed resource for communities in the early years of the civil rights movement. The church was one of the only Black-controlled community spaces and was the site of much organizing and recruitment. So, while many of the participants in the movement had multiple gendered barriers to their personal and structural availability (i.e. family obligations, working for unsympathetic whites, the need to be the breadwinner, lack of financial resources), the church was able to collectively offer a network of support to overcome those barriers.

In sum, networks are gendered by people's family roles and identities and serve as sites for potential recruitment. However, contact through a network is not enough to draw people into movements; they often need to hear or see examples of the movement's goals and beliefs to be drawn in.

Frames and Mobilization

One of the ways in which movement leaders reach out to the public is through an explanation of the movement's goals presented in a manner that captures people's attention. These can come in the form of slogans that provide information and, at the same time, politicize and legitimate the message. The hashtag Black Lives Matter is the use of a phrase that makes a statement that carries the political message of "we live in a society where Black lives don't matter." The political nature of this message can be seen in the almost immediate creation of counter frames such as "All Lives Matter" and "Blue Lives Matter." In another example, feminists in the 1980s wore buttons that read "59¢" as a way to inform the public and stir protests on wage inequality by pointing out the fact that women make 59¢ for every dollar a man makes. That button and #BlackLivesMatter are what social movement scholars call a *frame*, a politicized understanding of the movement's issues. As such, frames are a form of story, here "women make less money than men," that legitimates protest, consequently "the need to advocate for equal pay." Therefore, wearing the button is meant to educate and connect activists and potential participants (Hunt, Benford, and Snow 1994). In addition to making a claim legitimate, frames also seek to shift responsibility from knowledge to action. In doing so, they not only tell a story but compel the receiver to engage in action as a result.

Gendered frames

Frames can be gendered in their message, as illustrated by the example of the 59¢ button. The frame of "Black Lives Matter" was expanded through the creation of the gender-specific frame, "Say Her Name." This frame was articulated by Kimberlé Crenshaw and Andrea J. Ritchie as a way to note that Black cis- and transgender women's deaths at the hands of police did not receive the same attention as those of Black men. They write, "Neither these killings of Black women, nor the lack of accountability for them, have been widely lifted up as exemplars of the systemic police brutality that is currently the focal point of mass protest and policy reform" (2015). Here the frame of "Say Her Name," brings visibility to women killed and, at the same time, identifies the gender-specific risks Black women face in police encounters.

Overall, frames can be gendered in the same way that language and ideas in society are gendered. Verta Taylor notes that "it is not surprising that images of masculinity and femininity are reproduced in the language and ideas that social movement activists used to frame their messages and in the emotions they cultivate to mobilize and influence proponents and opponents" (1999: 21). These frames, like networks, are often drawn on traditional ideas of gender. For example, maternalism or the idea of motherhood has been a core frame for the environmental movement, just as it was for suffrage (McCammon et al. 2018). "Invoking motherhood as a rationale for women's activism also reveals continuity with an earlier generation of women suffrage advocates, who also argued that a political voice for women, including mothers, would lead to greater protections for children and family life" (2018: 322–323). When ideas of gender become attached to a movement, for example the risk-taking environmental activist (understood as masculine) or the nurturing organic farm proponent (understood as feminine), gender is also a part of the messages it sends to potential recruits.

Just like in "Say Her Name," movements may specifically imply gender in a frame. For example, Mothers Against Drunk Driving linked notions of motherhood to an issue that is not necessarily seen as connected to motherhood (i.e. drunk driving). The gendering of this frame, with the use of mothers, not only reaches out to other mothers, it also lends legitimacy to mothers as actors to address the issue. In similar ways to the campaign against drunk driving, there have been attempts to add gender to the Black Lives Matter framing of issues. Reflecting on the number of Black men killed in interactions with the police, *The Nation* writer Dani McClain calls on the reproductive justice movement, which traditionally has been associated with family planning and abortion, to take up the cause. McClain writes:

> With this most recent killing [Michael Brown, the 18-year-old killed in Ferguson, Missouri], I am wondering what it would take for more people in feminist and reproductive rights circles to begin to think of parents such as Lesley McSpadden, Sybrina Fulton, and Angela Leisure [mothers of men killed in interactions with the police] . . . as women they advocate for just as passionately and vigorously as they advocate for a young woman's right to contraception or an overwhelmed mother of three's right to an abortion. (McClain 2014)

In arguing for this connection, McClain links Black Lives Matter to the reproductive justice movement, and frames it as a gendered issue of caring for mothers as well as those seeking not to become mothers.

While the familiar notion of mothers as caring, nurturing, and the source of human reproduction can be linked to the needless deaths resulting from police brutality and drunk driving, movements may lose credibility if gender norms are stretched *too* far. "Activists who use gender in unfamiliar ways or otherwise violate gender expectations may find themselves delegitimated instead of the practices and arrangements that they challenge" (Einwohner et al. 2000: 692). For example, Rachel Einwohner (1999) studied animal rights movements and found that when the protestors were seen as feminine and emotional by hunters, the protests were not viewed as legitimate. In addition, while drawing on traditional gender norms, such as motherhood, can grant respectability to a movement, it can also serve to oversimplify issues and limit women to traditional roles (McCammon et al. 2018). As discussed in Chapter 2, too much reliance on traditional gender roles such as "mother" as seen in the Chilean women's movement can limit the spread of activism and accomplishment of movement goals.

While frames can legitimate participants in a movement such as mothers in Black Lives Matter, frames can also legitimate movement goals. How movement leaders use gender in framing can shape how valid their demands are viewed. For example, scholars Myra Marx Ferree and Silke Roth (1998) examined the issue of childcare in a West Berlin workers' strike. They found that a coalition that combined feminist efforts with labor could have framed childcare as something that benefits workers of all races and particularly those with lower incomes. Instead they found that the workers framed childcare as solely a "woman's" issue and not a "worker's" issue and limited its potential for success. Here the gendering of the frame as a women's issue delegitimized it as a goal in the workers' strike.

Even feminist organizations can frame gender in different ways. As discussed in Chapter 2, I found that motherhood was framed in two ways in a chapter of NOW (Reger 2001). One way was motherhood as a social status with political ramifications – that is, the world needs mothers to fix social problems, similar to Mothers Against Drunk Driving. This framing of motherhood made political action necessary and promoted the group's goals. The other was motherhood as an act of caring and taking responsibility for relationships. Here the focus was on consciousness-raising and support groups within the chapter. These two different framings co-existed within the chapter, situated in different settings. The overall result was a structure that allowed for members to find a home with either understanding and these interpretations were incorporated into frames extended to potential recruits. The result was the construction of distinct feminist identities within one organization.

Gendered mobilization

Just as frames can be gendered, so too can paths to mobilization. Mobilization results when a potential participant comes into contact with a movement through a network, is personally available, and finds the frames and goals of the movement compelling enough to engage in some form of activism. The Black Lives Matter protests in Portland, Oregon in the summer of 2020 are examples of this. Responding to the cry of George Floyd for his mother as he lay dying, women drew on the identity of mother in the protests, creating a "Wall of Moms" standing between the police and other protestors. The *New York Times* reported that at one July protest "[The moms dressed in yellow] link arm-in-arm, forming a human barricade between protestors and federal agents. Some wear respirators, gas masks, and helmets. Some hand out sunflowers. On one night of protests last week, they chanted, 'Feds stay clear! The moms are here!'" (Blum 2020). When the "Wall of Moms" was tear-gassed at protests, they were joined by a "Wall of Dads" who carried leaf blowers to send the tear gas back toward the police. Here, gendered frames drawing on "moms" and "dads" as compelling identities prompted mobilization. It is important to note that in a predominantly white city, these gendered identities also drew on white privilege in the interactions with police.

Another example of gendered mobilization is the participation of women in Brazilian squatter campaigns, studied by Kevin Neuhouser. Squatter campaigns seek to retain the right to houses built by impoverished people on unclaimed land and provide services to the communities there. Neuhouser (1995) found that in these multi-gender movements, women participated more, and were more likely to be mobilized, due to their adoption of traditional gender norms and family obligations. "Brazilian culture defines the domestic sphere as a female domain; therefore, poor urban women are highly motivated to secure access to those resources that are necessary for the reproduction of the household" (1995: 50). Movement goals focused on access to housing, water, and electricity, which aligned with the women's traditional division of labor. "Women were less likely than men to create formal organizational structures, relying instead on informal social exchange networks" (1995: 40–41). Pulled in by their need to care for the family, women's mobilization was inventive and expansive. "Women invaded land, built houses, resisted eviction, won access to water and electricity, and created a health post – all without generating a single social movement organization" (1995: 51). Overall, women used disruptive tactics more often than men and were more successful in attaining their collective goals because of their ability to be more spontaneous in their informal networks. However, because of the traditional norms that inspired their activism, the community largely did not credit the women with the changes they brought about.

In sum, the ways in which people are situated in society – the networks they have, the way they understand their gender, the contact they have with movement messages can all serve to shape how they become activists. They may draw on traditional ideas of gender to achieve their goals or challenge traditional norms. Once they enter movements, the identities they construct are also shaped by notions of gender.

Movement Identities

As noted in the introduction, developing a sense of "we" or connection as a group is an important dynamic of social movement organizations and communities. Verta Taylor and Nancy Whittier (1992) argue that activist identities are created through three processes. One process is the creation of boundaries between the activists and the outer society. This boundary can be as specific as targeting a specific group such as legislators, or as diffuse as contesting mainstream culture. Constructing boundaries helps to create a sense of who belongs in the group ("we") and who does not belong in the group ("they"). However, these boundaries cannot be impermeable. Activists must engage with some sort of negotiation with the target/enemy and the rest of society. It is here that actions such as protests, lobbying, and demonstrations are developed with the goal of making change, framing the goals of the movement and recruiting new members. Through interaction within the boundaries and negotiating outside of the group, a political consciousness is developed. Here what it means to be an activist becomes a key part of the participant's identities – one that has great meaning and can substantially guide their life. This sense of "we" is under constant construction and shifts as the movement changes over time.

All of these processes – boundary building, negotiation, and consciousness development – take place in a gendered world. Gender, along with race-ethnicity, class, nationality, religion, and other social statuses are factors in the development of activist identities. For example, in the case of the Mothers of the Plaza de Mayo who protested the disappearances of their sons and daughters, the role of mother brought them into the movement; however, once there, they began to develop the activist identity of the "grieved mother" seeking answers (Bosco 2006). In other words, gendered identity of *mother* brought them into the movement, but *activist mother* was the collective identity they created. Scholar Fernando Bosco describes that process:

> By sharing their sadness, anger, and frustration, and talking about ways in which they could collectively confront the problem, the mothers of the disappeared developed a collective identity: women who identified as mothers of the disappeared and who have met in the Plaza de Mayo or women who have heard about the mothers meeting in the plaza in Buenos Aires and started to refer to themselves in such terms. (2006: 351–352)

While the Madres de Plaza de Mayo clearly use gender in their movement, gender identities can be used to promote the goals of a movement whether or not it is specifically focused on gender. "Social movement actors often strategically claim or construct gendered identities to achieve their goals, whether or not those goals are explicitly gender related. In doing so, movement actors incorporate elements of cultural meanings about gender into their individual and collective identities and use those identities to lay claim to certain issues" (Einwohner et al. 2000: 687).

Within spaces such as social movement groups or communities, activists interact forming a shared consciousness on what it means to be in a movement. Group understandings of gender inequality, along with issues of class, race, and ethnicity, among others, can influence that consciousness, and consequently the activist identity. For example, part of identifying as a "feminist" is identifying who is a part of a community or organization and who is not, as well as coming to have a shared sense of the change that is sought in society (Reger 2012).

Shared activist or collective identities are more than attributes of the individual but are important elements to the group or community. For example, Leila Rupp and Verta Taylor (1987) argue that a gendered activist identity helped sustain the women's movement through the "doldrums" before its resurgence in the late 1960s. They found that in a hostile environment to feminism, members of the National Women's Party retreated into an "abeyance structure" (Taylor 1989) that kept their beliefs and identity alive, even though they did not make progress on their goals. Key to this survival was their shared history in the fight for suffrage, organizational headquarters that served as a home base, and close personal ties combined with a commitment to feminism. Likewise, in a more contemporary analysis, the women's movement in Great Britain has also been characterized as being in a state of abeyance with fewer national protests but not in a state of decline and still achieving some successes (Bagguley 2002).

Men's movements also construct gendered activist identities that incorporate other social identities such as class and race. The examples of the anti-war activist who burns his draft card, the "Wall of

Dads" participant who seeks to protect the "Wall of Moms," or the Freedom Summer campaign worker who does the high-risk community outreach, are all examples of an activist identity shaped by ideas of masculinity. Men bring ideas of masculinity to movements and also have their ideas of masculinity shaped by movements. The pro-feminist branch of the men's movement (discussed in Chapter 2) is an example of how men's ideas of what it means to be a man can change as activists interact and rethink gender norms.

In sum, gender can play a core role in the construction of an activist identity, shaping the boundaries of the group or community, its continuity, and its internal and external interactions. Taylor and Whittier (1992) detail how the gendered identity of "lesbian feminist" was constructed in communities across the United States in the 1970s and 1980s. Seeking to separate their lives from male domination and patriarchy, activist communities enacted boundaries between themselves and mainstream society. Parts of those boundaries were in the creation of separate women-focused institutions, such as health and rape crises centers, bookstores, martial arts groups, artist colonies, among others, and the "development of distinct women's cultures guided by 'female' values" in which men and women were seen as fundamentally different (1992: 112). As a result, lesbian feminist communities created spaces where the relationship between feminism, lesbianism, sexuality, and gender were reevaluated with the goal of being women-centered. "Being women-centered is viewed as challenging conventional expectations that women orient themselves psychologically and socially toward men, to compete with other women for male attention, and devalue other women" (1992: 119). As a result, lesbian feminist communities sought to remake traditional norms of femininity by adopting "non-traditional" forms of dress, behavior, and demeanor. Taylor and Whittier note:

> Challenging further the notion of femininity as frailty, passivity, and preoccupation with reigning standards of beauty, many women wear clothing that enables freedom of movement, adopt short or simple haircuts, walk with firm self-assured strides, and choose not to shave their legs or wear heavy makeup. (1992: 120)

In the course of constructing a collective identity, the gender identity of the participant can also change. A common strategy in the younger branch of the U.S. women's movement in the 1970s was to invite women into consciousness-raising sessions. These were sessions in which women would share experiences and concerns and come to see that their personal troubles were actually larger social issues. Often, while talking about relationships, sexual experiences, and everyday life, women became more radical in their views of gender and began to identify gender inequality in their lives versus accepting these experiences "as just the way things are." This process of realization was such a common experience that it became known as the "click," a moment when a woman came to understand that issues in her life were the result of gender inequality. *Ms.* magazine carried a reader's column for years filled with submitted stories about personal "clicks" that transformed consciousness and contributed to the construction of a feminist identity (Reger 2012). For example, one "click" moment read:

> Standing in line at the supermarket with my cart of groceries, a man with some crackers and a six-pack of beer cut in front of me without so much as a "May I?" I said, "Excuse me. I'm in line here." He looked at me and said, "I've only got two things." I replied, "Sorry." His response was a venomous and indignant "Bitch!" as he stormed off.
>
> "Click." After so many years, I got it. No matter how invisible, polite, or accommodating I am, someone's going to think I'm a bitch anyway, so I might as well embrace my own Inner Bitch and trot her out. There is absolutely no benefit in trying to be a non-bitch. (Snortland 2011)

When movement actors create a collective identity, issues can arise when what it means to be a member of the group is too closely aligned with a particular set of social identities. The U.S. women's movement is an example of groups, networks, and communities of feminists constructing an identity around the idea of the "universal woman," the view that all women have the same issues in common. While worldwide, women face many of the same issues of oppression and discrimination, the identity of "universal woman" ignores the diversity of women's experiences. Black feminist theorists and working-class and lesbian women argued that the mainstream feminist identity created was focused on white, middle-class heterosexual women, and missed the ways in which race-ethnicity, religion, class, sexual identity, among others, shaped experiences differently. This construction of a feminist identity that reflects only a portion of women continues to challenge current feminists who struggle to create diverse groups and networks (Reger 2012), and charges that feminism is still just for white women, continue into the twenty-first century. The women's marches of 2016, after the election of President Trump are an example of this continuing turmoil around identity and feminism. When the original march was organized, many balked at participating if it was only organized by white women. The organizing team was reconstituted to include a diverse set of women. That organizing team was later accused of antisemitism, resulting in another new group of leaders (Reger 2019).

As evidence of the importance of drawing on intersectionality in protest, the identity of "intersectional feminist" was prominent at the marches, with participants carrying signs such as "Intersectional Feminism Matters" and "If you don't fight for all women, you fight for NO women." Scholar Fátima Suárez (2019) documents the creation of the intersectional feminist identity and notes the importance of Chicana, Latina, and other women of color in its construction. Intersectionality is also key in Black Lives Matter. In the inception of the original hashtag at the death of Trayvon Martin, Alicia Garza drew on race as a primary motivator. Her thoughts on this were later captured in a news article:

> "The one thing I remember from that evening, other than crying myself to sleep that night, was the way in which, as a black person, I felt incredibly vulnerable, incredibly exposed, and incredibly enraged," Garza, then the special projects director of the National Domestic Workers Alliance in Oakland, Calif., said in recalling the day she saw the Zimmerman verdict pop up on Facebook. She was in a local bar with her husband, and they were surrounded by people disheartened by the news. She told the *Guardian* in 2015, "Seeing these black people leaving the bar, and it was like we couldn't look at each other.

We were carrying this burden around with us every day, of racism and white supremacy. It was a verdict that said: black people are not safe in America." (Finn 2020: online)

However, in the creation of a permanent group, the organizers specifically drew on a range of different social identities. "*We affirm the lives* of Black queer and trans folks, disabled folks, undocumented folks, folks with records, women, and all Black lives along the gender spectrum. Our network centers on those who have been marginalized within Black liberation movements (Black Lives Matter: online 2020 [emphasis in the original]).

While the identity created within the movement is critical to a social movement, so too is the way the identity is understood by those outside the movement. In the case of Black Lives Matter and the summer of 2020, a number of different images of protestors emerged. In some accounts, protestors were viewed as peaceful community members and in others, violent rioters destroying the community. Returning to an earlier example, the "Wall of Moms" – primarily made up of white women in the Portland protests – was a strategic attempt to control the image of the protests to those outside the movement.[3] These "identity interactions" between activists and bystanders and targets are shaped by race, class, gender, and other social identities. In Rachel Einwohner's analysis of two animal rights campaigns spearheaded by the same group of activists, she argues that the targets' conceptions of class and gender shaped the outcome of protests. She notes that although animal rights is a multi-gender movement, middle-class women make up the majority of participants. She studied two of the group's campaigns – one protesting the cruelty of circuses, and the other focused on hunting as a "cruel ... blood sport" (1999: 62). During the circus campaign, activists held demonstrations outside the circus distributing flyers and holding signs that read "Your ticket promotes cruelty" and "Circus animals are sold into slavery ..." (1999: 60). Attendance figures at area circuses dropped after the group started to protest. In the campaign against hunting, the activists sent letters to state officials as well as "hunt sabs" (saboteurs), meant to disrupt hunting. In the "hunting sabs," activists approached hunters with the goal of educating them on the use of public land, animal rights, and vegetarianism. The hunting campaign had limited success and, ultimately, did not achieve what they wanted. To explain the difference between the two campaigns, Einwohner argues that it was not the form of protest – demonstrations vs. letter writing and approaching hunters – but instead how the targets viewed the activists. The hunters largely found the activists' views to be misguided and uninformed, and drawing on emotion instead of logic. Overall, the hunters viewed the activists as having "a set of stereotypical feminist characteristics" and saw them as middle-class "office workers" who know nothing of animals and the outdoors (1999: 67). On the other hand, she found that circus patrons viewed the animal rights activists through a lens as "kooks" "uneducated on animals" or in the most gendered way as "caring people," or "very gentle, sweet types" who are "trying to change things for the good of animals" (1999: 69). In sum, the circusgoers did not make the same class and gender assumptions as did the hunters. She concludes that an intersectional analysis of the gendered and class identities of the activists shaped how credible and legitimate their claims were.

Overall, how people come to movements is one of gendered processes. People are situated in gendered networks; they are drawn in through gendered frames and become active in gendered routes of mobilization. Once in movements or movement organizations, people interact to construct activist identities, drawing on gender as well as other social identities. Key to all these processes of coming to a movement is the connection between gender and emotion.

Emotions and Movements

In societies that use gender as a sorting mechanism, the presumption of a gender binary also extends to the gendering of emotions. Indeed, many of the notions supporting the gender binary include the idea that men and women are emotionally different from each other. Overall, women are viewed as more emotional and men as more logical or rational (as documented in Einwohner's animal rights study). Alison Jaggar (1989) identifies this as a dichotomy with emotion, seen as feminine, as lesser than the rational, which is seen as masculine. She writes:

> Not only has reason been contrasted with emotion, but it has also been associated with the mental, the cultural, the universal, the public, and the male, whereas emotions have been associated with the irrational, the physical, the natural, the particular, the private, and, of course, the female. (1989: 145)

While emotions might be seen as feminine overall, gender scholars note that emotions themselves are gendered. Masculine emotions such as expressing anger or fury are often more active and valued, versus feminine emotions such as expressing grief or depression. Stephanie Shields and her co-authors (2006) argue that people "do emotions," just as they "do" gender (West and Zimmerman 1987). In sum, to do one's gender also means to do the appropriate emotions.

Doing gendered emotions

Social movements also "do emotions" just as they "do gender." How emotions are done in movements often differs between men and women. Women's emotions are often labeled deviant and ineffective, and movements work to transform them into something more effective. Men's emotions, when they are studied, are often seen as justified and useful for movement recruitment and mobilization. For example, in her study of Australian feminists, Cheryl Hercus (1999) argues that women's anger and feminism are seen as deviant in society and lead to labels such as "man haters." To deal with this sense of deviance, women used self-restraint when talking about feminist ideas or beliefs. She concludes the costs of this emotion work could be both negative in the form of exhaustion, guilt, and self-estrangement, or positive with women experiencing a sense of freedom and self-affirmation. Her work illustrates how anger, seen as deviant for women, can be channeled to make social change.

Audre Lorde in her essay, "The Uses of Anger," on fighting racism, elaborates on how emotions such as anger and rage can be channeled when women are not afraid to use them. She writes:

> Any discussion among women about racism must include the recognition and the use of anger. It must be direct and creative, because it is crucial. We cannot allow our fear of anger to deflect us nor to seduce us into settling for anything less than the hard work of excavating honesty; we must be quite serious about the choice of this topic and the angers entwined within it, because, rest assured, our opponents are quite serious about their hatred of us and of what we are trying to do here. (1997: 281)

Drawing on #MeToo and women's reports of harassment and abuse (as described in the introduction), Rebecca Hussey in a review of books coming out in 2018 noted, "Anger is in the air, and with good reason. If ever there was a time for unruly women, this is it." Books published included Brittney Cooper's *Eloquent rage: A Black feminist discovers her superpower* (St. Martin's Press), Soraya Chemaly's *Rage becomes her: The power of women's anger* (Atria Books) and Rebecca Traister's *Good and bad: The revolutionary power of women's anger* (Simon and Schuster). Key to all of these titles is that anger is an underused source of women's empowerment.

In addition to how activists view and negotiate emotion, movement participants can be viewed through the lens of gender. Returning to the hunters in Einwohner's study of animal rights activists, we can see that they found the mostly female activists to be emotional versus logical, and dismissed their claims. Yet the mostly male hunters expressed this through emotions such as anger at the activists, finding their actions "maddening" (1999: 74). Here, emotion is used to dismiss the (women) activists but confirm the view of the (men) targets. This case illustrates how when emotion is perceived on both sides of the equation, it is men's anger that is viewed as rational and legitimate, supporting the concept of the gendered emotion binary.

Emotions can pull people into movements and help to mobilize action (Aminzade and McAdam 2001). For example, Mary

Cappelli examines the emotion in the graffiti around the death of George Floyd in the Black Lives Matter protests and finds that different themes "represent the evolution of time, thought, and emotions" (2020: 89). She sees a transition in the messages from a desire to overthrow existing institutions such as "Defund the Police," to one of fear and remembrance as in "Say their Names" and "Am I Next?" to a hopefulness that change is possible seen in "Love Prevails" and "Together We Rise." Each of these messages draws on a different set of emotions – rage, grief, and fear to hope and love. In the case of the Madres de Plaza de Mayo, emotions of "reciprocal affection" helped in the emergence, continuity, and sustaining of their network. This emotional labor was so successful that the Madres de Plaza de Mayo went from a local network riddled with disagreements to a global network with support groups around the world (Bosco 2006).

Indeed, Jeff Goodwin, James Jasper, and Francesca Polletta (2001) argue that love and hate are strong, sustained emotions that can bring people into a movement. When events or situations trigger a strong reaction in individuals, called "moral shocks," they can be propelled to action (Jasper 1998). Moral shocks are similar to "hot cognition," where individuals recognize inequality coupled with intense emotion (Gamson 1992). Both can bring people into movements. For example, in the 1990s, a major "moral shock" and moment of "hot cognition" inspiring women's anger was the televised Clarence Thomas Supreme Court nomination hearings. Many women were incensed that Anita Hill, his former law clerk, had her charges of sexual harassment dismissed and her reputation ruined. As a result of these emotions, women's rights organizations saw an increase in members and participation. Emotional connections to places, people, and issues can draw people into movements. In her study of women leaders in the civil rights movement, Belinda Robnett (1997) found that emotions were important in sustaining activism. She argues that women activists built intimate relationships with people at the grassroots level and this emotional connection kept communities mobilized.

Once in a social movement, activist identities are often constructed around emotions. Strong emotions such as love and respect can become a part of the collective identity of the group, solidifying the sense of connection and being a part of "we." However, strong negative emotions can also shape activist identities. Hercus (1999) in her study of Australian feminists examined how they often framed their experiences around anger. She found that women constructed a feminist identity infused with anger when they began to recognize male domination, the oppression of women, and their lost opportunities. Women activists have also used traditional gender norms around emotions to engage in high-risk activism (Aminzade and McAdam 2001). For instance, in Argentina, women whose children have been "disappeared" by the government used grief as a tactic to protest publicly. Drawing sympathy from bystanders, the Madres de Plaza de Mayo avoided repressive reactions by the state because of emotional values associated with motherhood. In sum, being grieving mothers allowed them to resist the state and its repressive tactics.

This work of channeling emotions is the result of "emotion cultures" that exist within movements, which allow participants to redefine feeling and expression rules (Taylor 1996, 2000). For example, in her study of postpartum depression, Verta Taylor (2000) found that support groups served as emotion cultures and worked to redefine women's expected emotional responses by allowing them to express feelings at odds with notions of motherhood. She notes, "In 'speaking out' about the guilt, anxiety, depression, anger – even the psychosis – connected with motherhood, postpartum depression activists challenge the emotion norms that support the maternal role" (2000: 277).

Activists not only respond to and have emotions, they also use emotions strategically to signal ideas about themselves to each other and to outsiders (Goodwin, Jasper, and Polletta 2001). Returning to Cappelli's study of graffiti, she finds that the image of the clenched fist extended upwards has been used as a symbol for Black liberation from the civil rights movement to Black Lives Matter (2020). Movement participants drew on this imagery as a way to quickly communicate feelings of rage and resistance. In the global Occupy movement, the word "Occupy" was chosen for its emotional power. Jenny Pickerill and John Krinsky note that "*to occupy* had a stronger and more controversial implication than simply to set up camp or hold a sit in. This use of powerful language as a tactical choice which framed the movement in a certain way ..." (2015: 3).

Understanding how activists use emotions to communicate can change perceptions of protestors as the "angry, out of control mob" to viewing them as strategically employing emotions to accomplish a goal. This work of managing and transforming emotions is called "emotion work," channeling emotions to accomplish a goal (Hochschild 1983). For example, movement leaders try to inspire emotions in followers to keep the movement going (Goodwin, Jasper, and Polletta 2001). In a study of transgender social movement organizations, Douglas Schrock and his co-authors (2004) found that leaders used messages that promised emotional harmony to draw in participants who struggled with feelings of fear, shame, powerlessness, and alienation. Participants can also sing, chant, or engage in rituals to inspire certain emotional responses such as an increase in a sense of connection in the group to sustain activism. In many Black Lives Matter demonstrations, protestors were asked to kneel for 8 minutes and 46 seconds – the time George Floyd had Officer Derek Chauvin's knee pressed against his neck – as a symbolic and emotional way of educating and uniting the activists. In addition to using emotions to push the movement forward, activists may purposely try to goad their targets into responding with inappropriate emotions such as fear, surprise, anger, and disgust as ways to reduce their power or make them appear as illegitimate actors (Goodwin, Jasper, and Polletta 2001).

Movements can also work to transform emotions. This is called "emotional socialization" that teaches participants the "feeling rules" or emotional guidelines of the group and promotes unified activism. I found that in the New York City chapter of NOW, which began running consciousness-raising groups to address the demands of incoming members (Reger 2004). Consciousness raising, the process by which women gather together on a regular basis to discuss their personal lives and experiences in an egalitarian, leaderless group setting, became a core part of the chapter through the creation of a committee. In the committee, women are encouraged to explore their common experiences with gender inequality and then act. This process was very emotional, with two primary emotions expressed by the women – anger or rage, resulting from a moral shock and a sense of alienation, or loneliness because of their life situations or their feminist beliefs. Both emotions had gendered components. By providing women with a space to discuss their lives, the committee facilitates the emotion work that allows women to explore commonalities, share information, create new perceptions, and validate their emotions. Although the process often leaves women angry, there is a fundamental shift in this shared emotion when it is validated. As a social change agent, NOW works to direct this anger into political activism.

While NOW uses collective emotions to make change, the use of individual emotions can also be used to accomplish movement goals. To advance the goals of Black Lives Matter, the mothers of Michael Brown, Trayvon Martin, Sandra Bland, Eric Garner, and five others came forward to tell their stories at the 2016 Democratic National Convention. Dubbed the "Mothers of the Movement," their stories promoted the chant of "Black Lives Matter!" to break out in the crowd (Kaleem 2016). While the "Mothers of the Movement" spoke together telling their stories, activists can stand alone, telling their stories for change. For example, in her study of the child sexual abuse movement, Nancy Whittier (2001) notes that the emotional labor of an individual telling a rape or abuse story in public can be used as a means of social change and can become a part of an organization's strategy. This is a similar strategy to the LGBTQ+ movement's strategy of "coming out" as a way to dispel the shame and internalized homophobia of the individual, as well as make social change through visibility.

In sum, doing emotions is also doing gender in social movements, and this is often filtered through the gender binary. Interwoven through the forces that bring people into social movement and mobilize them are emotions and gender. Messages extended to potential participants can draw on our understanding of gender and emotions by offering solutions to gender and emotional deviance in the form of transformation. Identities are constructed in social movements that are gendered, as well as draw on emotions, and emotions are key to the processes that create a sense of "we" in movements. It is important to note that much of the research on gender, emotions and social movements has been focused on women. The lack of examples of men's emotionality in movements and how it is transformed or accommodated again tells us that too often men are left out of these conversations – constructed as simply "activists" ignoring the gender component of emotional connection to movements.

Conclusion

Overall, using the example of Black Lives Matter and other movements, this chapter explores how people come to social movements, why they come, and how they become active. Gender plays a key role in all of these processes: First, the manner in which gender sorts the work we do in families and in work and careers shapes our personal availability, the level of risk we assume in actions, and how we view the stigma associated with being an activist. Second, the networks we belong to are also shaped by gender and can educate us and pull us into social movements. These gendered networks often pre-exist movements and are made up of like-minded people. In the case of Black Lives Matter, we can see how Facebook and Twitter were the sites that connected many pre-existing networks, bringing people out to the 2020 protests. Third, the messages movements project – or frames – can have gendered dimensions that can attract (such as a feminist message on women's income inequality) or detract (such as animal rights activists being viewed as emotional and uninformed) from a movement. Fourth, how people become mobilized is also gendered. That was evident in the 2020 Portland Black Lives Matter protests; the "Wall of Dads" showed up after the "Wall of Moms" was teargassed. Fifth, the collective identities constructed within movements are shaped by gender as well as other social identities like race-ethnicity, social class, age, and others. Understandings of gender can be transformed into activism as evidenced by the Madres de Plaza de Mayo turning grief into action. Finally, just as emotions are gendered in everyday life, they are also gendered in social movements. Gendered emotions play multiple roles in movements and are shaped by the gender binary that sorts social life. Emotions pull people into movements, are transformed within movements and can be used to dismiss the work of movements. In sum, gender moves beyond the individual activist and plays a key role in the forces and process that bring people to a movement. I next turn in Chapter 4 to how gender is integrated into the strategies, tactics, and outcomes of activism.

Sources to Explore

Chatelain, Marcia and Kaavya Asoka. 2015. Women and Black Lives Matter. *Dissent* 63: 3: 54–61

Crenshaw, Kimberlé W. and Andrea J. Ritchie (with Rachel Anspach and Rachel Gilmer). 2015. *Say her name.* African American Policy Forum, Center for Intersectionality and Social Policy Studies, New York.

Goodwin, Jeff, James Jasper, and Francesca Polletta (eds.). 2001. *Political passions: Emotions and social movements.* Chicago: University of Chicago Press.

Mobilizing Ideas, a blog by the Center for Social Movements at the University of Notre Dame. https://mobilizingideas.wordpress.com/

Politics Outdoors, a blog by Dr. David Meyer, University of California-Irvine. https://politicsoutdoors.com/

Taylor, Verta. 1996. *Rock-a-by baby: Feminism, self-help and postpartum depression.* New York: Routledge.

Questions to Consider

1. What networks do you belong to? How could social movement activists work to draw you in using these networks?

2. Consider some of the current social movements going on around you today. Can you identify the frames that are being used? Are any of these gendered frames?
3. What are the three processes necessary for the construction of a collective identity? How can gender be a part of each of these processes?
4. How does the lens of intersectionality change or complicate our views of activists' identities?
5. Pick an emotion and discuss how it can be seen as gendered in your society. How could this emotion become a part of a social movement's identity, or frame?

Reflection

Do you think there is still a gendered emotion binary in society? Can you think of an example to either refute or support this from your own life and experiences?

4

*Guiding Social Change:
When Gender Shapes
Movement Trajectories*

Wheeling-Pittsburgh Steel, Steubenville, Ohio.
Credit: Harald Finster

It is late summer in 1985. The steelworkers at Local 1190 at Wheeling-Pittsburgh Steel in Steubenville, Ohio have been on strike since July. Although women work at the plant, only one woman is on the union's executive committee. Seasoned activist Cecelia Humienny struggles to have the men on the committee take her seriously. Forgetting to invite her to meetings, they also ignore her suggestions and ideas. Frustrated, she does not give up but instead finds a way to suggest her ideas to one of her male colleagues so that he can bring it forward. After they disregard her suggestion to start a food bank, she decides to organize one anyway without the men's support. Humienny isn't alone in struggling to participate in a meaningful way. The striking workers have two main duties assigned to them – either kitchen duty or picket line. Some of the women, finding that they were the ones primarily assigned to the kitchen, began to refuse the work. Instead, they want to work on the more visible and solidarity-building picket line with the men, despite the danger. The women lucky enough to work on the picket line find that men dropped some of the "male posturing" from the mill and interact with women co-workers in a more authentic way. As the strike progresses, it is the unemployment committee, headed by Humienny, that connects a broad coalition of business, banking, labor, religious, civil rights, educational, and government interests. Under her leadership, the committee is able to transition from helping unemployed workers before the strike to fundraise, advocate, and aid the striking workers.

Summarized from Fonow (1998)

Strikes, like social movements, are a form of collective action where gender continues to play a role. Where movement leaders may have drawn on ideas of gender and gendered networks to bring people into movements – once in a movement – gender shapes what participants do to accomplish their goals. This shaping of actions within a movement is called working within a "gendered political context" (Holly McCammon et al. 2001). In the scenario of the striking steelworkers, Mary Margaret Fonow (1998) documents how gender shapes the context of the strike, influencing experiences and the actions of the workers. The strike illustrates several important ways that gender guides social change. First, who is seen as an "appropriate" leader is gendered, with women often being passed over. Cecelia Humienny accomplished much for the workers but was shut out of recognized leadership.

Second, when women are bypassed as "official" leaders, they still find ways to lead and make change. For example, Humienny, struggling to be seen as legitimate within organizing circles, moved her activism to outside of the executive committee. Third, we can also see how actions, such as picketing and providing food, are gendered as well as the overall ideas and plans that guide these actions, such as educating the public on the issues, and supporting the workers. Taking the steelworkers' strike as an example, we can see how in the kitchen and on the picket line, the division of labor remains gendered. Fourth, we can see how gendered ideas can be contested and changed. Women rejected the kitchen for the picket line and, when they got there, men came to view them in a different light. All of these dynamics happen in a gendered political context as people seek to make social change.

Finally, as we have seen with other areas of social movements, gender intertwines with other social identities to shape how people fare and function. This is particularly apparent with leadership. In this chapter, I examine how movement leadership is shaped by gender and how feminist scholars rework the concept of a leader to include other social identities such as race-ethnicity. I then explore how gender influences a movement's actions, plans, and outcomes.

Gender and Leadership

Social movement scholars agree that leaders are essential to (but understudied in) social movements. Drawing on a review of the literature, Aldon Morris and Suzanne Staggenborg define leaders as "strategic decision-makers" who bring people into movements, inspire, and organize them (2004: 171). Leaders are different from organizers in that they are held accountable for their decisions by members and, as strategic decision-makers, they survey the social environment and decide the best course of action. Leaders are some of the most powerful people in an organizational hierarchy and gender shapes organizational leadership. Just as Doug McAdam (1988) in his examination of Freedom Summer (in Chapter 2) noted, men and women tend to do different jobs and fill different roles in social movements. Leadership is one of those roles. Just as men are often seen as the "default" activists in social movements, they are also often seen as the appropriate people to assume leadership roles. Morris and Staggenborg support this observation and note that leaders are "disproportionately male, and usually share the race or ethnicity of their supporters" (2004: 174.) Because leadership implies hierarchy, people in movements have different levels of power; leaders having more power than followers. Hierarchy and power differences often have gendered components (Kuumba 2001). Scholar M. Bahati Kuumba notes that "in gender-integrated movements, patriarchal assumptions are often superimposed on this hierarchical conception of leadership, creating a gender split in movement roles and leadership patterns" (2001: 80). We can see this split in story of the organizing of the steelworkers' strike that opens this chapter. While Humienny's work was essential to the survival of the striking workers, she was shut out of more formal organizing by the men around her.

One result of this gender split can be seen in the organizing of communities. Susan Stall and Randy Stoecker (1998) argue that much of the work that goes into social movements happens at the community level – and gender shapes organizations and communities. They call this kind of organizing the women-centered model and argue that it builds on the ways in which women form and maintain relationships within their communities. "Within the women-centered model, [there is] the maintenance and development of personal connections with others that provide a safe environment for people to develop, change, and grow ..." (1998: 740). Returning again to the steelworkers' strike, it was Humienny's work in the community before the strike that enabled the union to take care of the striking workers. She was able to build a coalition of local organizations and institutions precisely because she was embedded and worked within the community.

While Stall and Stoecker see community organizing as more feminine or women-centered, feminists have viewed traditional leadership hierarchies in titles such as president, vice president, chairman, and others as patriarchal. As a result, women's movement activists often seek to create organizations that do not replicate the more "masculine" hierarchy of formal organizations (Thomas 1999). Women's movement groups, particularly in the reemergence of the U.S. women's movement, sought to create more decentralized groups based on personal networks with a more fluid leadership in the 1960s and 1970s. The Miss America protest scenario, which opened Chapter 1, was organized by radical feminists who adopted an anti-hierarchal, decentralized group structure to avoid a more patriarchal model. Their groups were often labeled as leaderless. While these perspectives on leadership focus on changing gender dynamics, civil rights movement research illustrates how race-ethnicity and class, along with gender, are an important lens to examine leadership dynamics.

> Across history, any time a movement has had black women at its helm or in its leadership – from Ida B. Wells and the Niagara movement to Ella Baker in the civil rights movement – there have been sexist and racist attempts to undermine them. The most damaging impact of the sanitized and oversimplified version of the civil rights story is that it has convinced many people that single, charismatic male leaders are a prerequisite for social movements. This is simply untrue. (Chatelain 2015: 58)

The civil rights movement in the United States is a rich site for scholars to explore gender, social class, and race in leadership. Feminist scholar Bernice McNair Barnett argues that women in the civil rights movement played vital roles that were not identified by men as leadership. She argues that is due to the triple constraints of gender, race, and social class. "Although seldom recognized as leaders, these women were often the ones who initiated protest, formulated strategies and tactics, and mobilized other resources (especially money, personnel, and communication networks) necessary for successful collective action" (1993: 163). Charles Payne in his study of women activists summarizes their status, noting that it looks as though "men led, but women organized." "The everyday maintenance of the movement [by women] is effectively devalued, sinking beneath the level of our sight" (Payne 1990: 165). Barnett finds the same dynamics in her research. She writes:

The roles that they performed, whether at the grass-roots level or behind the scenes, represent profiles in courage and suggest that they were *leaders* in their communities, *leaders* in the day-to-day fight against various forms of oppression, and *leaders* in the modern civil rights movement. (1993: 177 [emphasis in the original])

Belinda Robnett (1997) builds on these observations and expands on women's "invisible leadership" with the conceptualization of "bridge leadership." Bridge leadership, she argues, was done by women in the civil rights movement who did not have formal positions within social movement organizations but instead served as vital links between the group and the community. Robnett states, though undervalued in the movement, bridge leadership was the cornerstone of much of the movement's mobilization and played a role in its successes. Women such as JoAnn Robinson, Septima Poinsette Clark, McCree Harris, Shirley Sherrod, Diane Nash, Johnnie Carr, Thelma Glass, and Georgia Gilmore did important work in the movement but were not recognized because of a focus on a more masculine, status-oriented leadership. While Barnett and Robnett's work added new dimensions to the study of gender and leadership, they also drew attention to the ways in which social movement theories and scholarship need an intersectional perspective that moves beyond a white, middle-class, male focus. However, when women do become recognized leaders, they can face barriers and hostility.

The Case of Occupy

In September 2011, a small group of activists camped out in Manhattan's Zuccotti park to protest the inequalities arising from a capitalistic economic and political system. Brought together through the organizing efforts of a team at Adbusters, a Canadian-based activist media collective, participants learned about the protest through email, websites and the hashtag OCCUPYWALLSTREET on Twitter (Occupy Wall Street 2019). The key issue was how the "economic system is rigged for the very few while the majority continue to fall behind" (Levitin 2015: online). Overall Occupy is described as

A leaderless resistance movement with people of many colors, genders, and political persuasions. The one thing we all have in common is that We Are The 99% that will no longer tolerate the greed and corruption of the 1%. We are using the revolutionary Arab Spring tactic [creating a protest encampment] to achieve our ends and encourage the use of nonviolence to maximize the safety of all participants. (Occupy Wall Street 2019)

The protests included setting up encampments in town parks, sharing food and lodgings, holding rallies and marches, and developing extensive social media. The Wall Street protest quickly spread to 82 countries and gave rise to a new language, one that identified inequality through the frame of the 99% versus the 1%. While Occupy varied in each context and its Western origins meant it did not always transfer well to some countries, it did have an international reach achieved through the internet (Pickerill and Krinsky 2015). Some credit the protests as highlighting the need for a higher minimum wage in the United States, as well as key issues in the environmental movement such as the Keystone XL pipeline that has been the focus of multiple protests and issues of policing and protest, among others (Levitin 2015).

While Occupy describes itself as a leaderless organization, leaders did emerge in the different Occupy sites. Scholar Heather Hurwitz (2019) found that leaders emerged through their relationships with others as they organized, and others followed. She calls this form of leadership relational, established through interaction and done without titles. Hurwitz also found that when women and genderqueer (i.e. those who choose to identify outside of the gender binary) people took up the role of leader, they faced hostility and barriers. Hurwitz finds that to discourage women and genderqueer leaders, followers used forms of "discriminatory resistance" that included the "double bind" which expects women leaders to be both feminine *and* aggressive as leaders, and a "leadership labyrinth" that included "harassment, male dominance, and a hostile culture" (2019: 158–159). Women and genderqueer leaders met resistance in a variety of ways. Hurwitz documents how some struggled to convince the group of issues until men echoed their concerns. Others had men speak over them even when they had the role of facilitator and members in the crowd urged the man to "let her speak." Women leaders recalled instances of having intoxicated men physically and sexually harass them while other Occupy participants looked on (2019: 167). In one incident, Artemis, a young woman of mixed-race background recalled trying to lead a general assembly meeting. "There was no security, so anyone who wanted to could run up to the stage and get up in my face. Visibly intoxicated men were leering at me and I was like, 'This is a hot mess!' It was overwhelming" (quoted in Hurwitz, 2019: 167). Hurwitz concludes, "When followers act implicitly or explicitly on the stereotype that elite white men are the ideal leaders, they fail to cooperate with – and can even sabotage – women and genderqueer leaders, particularly people of color" (158).

Contributing to the treatment of leaders was an overall environment that made hostility and dominance a part of the culture. These forms of discrimination not only drew on ideas of gender but also race when followers "implicitly or explicitly" embraced racial and gendered prejudices (2019: 160). The first issue of the feminist 'zine [DIY magazine] called *Workin' On It! We Activate! We Agitate! Womyn of Color Occupy Wall Street & Beyond* documented everyday resentment directed at women of color and transgender Occupy activists. "Many of us experienced or witnessed slurs, attacks . . . When we attempted to challenge these abuses, we were silenced or ostracized . . . we have identified a shadow leadership structure . . . The result is heightened anxiety and/or suspicion of women of color and/or queer voices who challenge organizing practices" (2019: 171).

Overall, two key points on gender and leadership are illustrated. First, feminist scholars argued that the lack of women in leadership positions is the result of how leadership is defined. Too often, they argue that conceptions of leadership are created through a narrow, gendered lens as opposed to recognizing the diversity of leadership forms and styles. Robnett's conception of "bridge" versus "invisible" leadership illustrates this redefining (1997). Second, even when women and genderqueer people do find ways to assume leadership roles, Hurwitz's work illustrates how notions of gender and race can work against them when followers engage in discriminatory resistance and create a hostile environment (2019).

While some scholars have worked to rewrite gendered notions of leadership, other scholars examined how gender can be at the heart of protest actions. When movement leadership propose forms of activism, these are called tactics. Tactics can be a part of a repertoire or package, that movement groups and organizations draw on to achieve their goals. Tactics and tactical repertoires are shaped by the strategies that movements endorse. Strategies are the plans and form that tactics support or as Marshall Ganz puts it "Strategy is how we turn what we have into what we need – by translating our resources into the power to achieve purpose" (2000: 1010). As they guide social change, tactics and strategies can be gendered.

Gendered Strategies

Movements actors articulate both strategies and tactics in their effort to achieve their goals. Strategies are how movements plan their timing, targets, and tactics (Ganz 2000). Returning to Wheeling-Pittsburgh Steel in 1985 that opened this chapter, the strategy employed by the union was for there to be a work stoppage in the form of a strike. That strike was supported by a range of tactics, including using the threat of violence to keep others from taking up the work. However, other social movement strategies are specifically built around non-violence. For instance, many civil rights organizations embraced non-violent civil disobedience to channel their actions. This was a strategy that had the potential to de-escalate violence by not responding with violence. The strategy has had its roots in the movement led by Mahatma Gandhi, who endorsed non-violence in campaigns seeking India's independence from British colonial rule. Civil disobedience is the refusal to abide by a particular law or policy that is identified as discriminatory and problematic. Therefore, the strategy of non-violent civil disobedience is a plan (e.g. refusing to engage in violence while working to change laws and policies) with coordinated actions against targets at specific times. Strategies carry with them symbolic meanings as well as strategic plans. Symbolically, embracing non-violent civil disobedience portrayed civil rights activists as different from the virulent hatred and racism they faced in white communities, while at the same time, it provided a plan of action for making change.

Sociologist Arlie Hochschild argues that all strategies can be gendered. In her study of families, she defined a gendered strategy as "a plan of action through which a person tries to solve problems at hand, given the cultural notions of gender at play" (1989: 15). In Hochschild's research, the issue was how to divide the household division of labor among men and women. She argues that in our everyday life, people draw on gendered beliefs that are often learned in childhood and reinforced through emotions. Just as the way in which people approach the household division of labor and the workforce with gender strategies, so too do activists with the tasks they seek to accomplish. Pamela Sugiman (1992), in her study of a United Auto Workers (UAW) strike in Canada, finds that gendered division in the workplace results in gendered strategies for social change. She argues:

> A strategy is not simply a calculated plan of action. Rather, it is an approach based on a configuration of emotional responses, patterned behaviours, intellectual assertions, and reasoned decisions. Insofar as men and women are gendered subjects who occupy distinct positions in society, and who thereby face different opportunities and constraints, they approach and contest the workplace in gendered ways. (1992: 3)

Sugiman observes that the UAW strike strategies became gendered when women workers politicized the role of women, focusing on the misconceptions that ignored women's financial role in the family and treated them as non-essential workers who did not deserve to be in an all-male environment. In doing so, they separated the women's experiences from the sense of industrial unionism which espoused that all workers were treated equally. Instead, she writes, "Central to [the women workers'] campaign was the message that women have a place in the UAW and that they should therefore use the union as a vehicle to achieve gender equality" (1992: 17). Pressing their desire for equality between all workers, the women won the removal of gender distinctions in the workforce and were viewed equally with men.

Women in the Wheeling-Pittsburgh Steel strike also drew on gender in their support of the strike. They both complied with gender norms by doing activities like staffing the kitchens to feed the striking workers and also transgressed them by asserting their right to be on the picket line, facing danger and violence, the same as the men.

Code Pink anti-war demonstration.
Credit: Ben Schumin/Flickr

Strategies can be gendered through the use of ideas and norms associated with gender. In the early 2000s, Rachel Kutz-Flamenbaum studied feminist anti-war organizations that drew on ideas of gender in their protests (2007). Some of the groups aligned their strategies with traditional gender norms while others pushed against them. She found that in the groups Code Pink and Raging Grannies traditional notions of femininity are employed. Code Pink uses the feminine color of pink added to the phrase "Code Blue," used to indicate a hospital emergency to signal. Together "code pink" signals an urgent need to end war from a women's perspective. The phrase also reflects the idea of getting a "pink slip" and losing a job. This is focused at the politicians who continue to support war. One of the first actions was a four-month vigil in 2002 outside the White House. The organizers described this start:

> CODEPINK thus emerged out of a deep desire by a group of American women to stop the United States from invading Iraq. The name CODEPINK plays on the former Bush Administration's color-coded homeland security alerts – yellow, orange, red – that signaled terrorist threats. While [President George W.] Bush's color-coded alerts were based on fear and were used to justify violence, the CODEPINK alert is a feisty call for people to "wage peace." (CODEPINK 2019: online)

Another group, the Raging Grannies, who work for peace, justice, and economic and social equality, through their name, also draw on gender. As discussed in Chapter 3, rage is an emotion that is often gendered masculine; while "grannies" are perceived as harmless, kind, and gentle. Together "Raging" and "Grannies"

Raging Grannies.
Credit: s pants/Flickr

provide a cognitive jolt that mixes gendered ideas in an unexpected manner. The organizers describe their philosophy as such:

> The delights of grannying include: dressing like innocent little old ladies so we can get close to our "target," writing songs from old favourites that skewer modern wrongs, satirizing evil-doing in public and getting everyone singing about it, watching a wrong back down and turn tail and run, sharing a history with other women who know who they are and what they're about. Grannying is the least understood yet most powerful weapon we have. Sometimes, looking back, we can see grannying was the only thing that could have met the need. (Raging Grannies 1987: online)

Missile Dick Chicks.
Credit: Steve Rainwater/Flickr

The third group Kutz-Flamenbaum studied – Missile Dick Chicks – takes a different approach and transgresses gender norms satirically by creating a performance of women who are pro-war. These pro-war women are portrayed as ridiculous and male identified. In their name and street theater, the members adorn themselves with penises ("dicks") and present themselves as "chicks." Focused on protesting the presidency of President George H. Bush, people are encouraged to join if they believe:

- You must be forever committed to keeping our CEO in the White House, along with his l'il Commander In Chief (that's Dick 'n' Bush, in case you didn't know!).
- Daddies are important! Either your real Daddy or your Sugar Daddy needs to be connected to Big Oil, Auto, or Wartime Wealth – who do you think's gonna buy your boob job, not to mention your missile?
- You must wear your hair Just Right: red, white, or blue, or red-white-AND-blue all together. (Missile Dick Chicks no date: online)

The Missile Dick Chicks are not the only groups to transgress gender norms in their strategies, historically women's movements have drawn on transgressive strategies when other means to equality are blocked. For instance, British activist Emmeline Pankhurst is known for forming the radical women's group, Women's Social and Political Union, to work for suffrage in 1903. Known as the first activists to be called suffragettes, Pankhurst, her daughter and followers engaged in an "unfeminine" strategy of violence to achieve the right to vote with tactics such as window smashing and arson. When sent to jail, Pankhurst engaged in hunger strikes and was violently force-fed. When she remained too weak, she was let out of jail until she regained her strength and then was sent back to prison where she again went on a hunger strike. Her activism for suffrage was interrupted by the First World War and just before her death in 1928, British women of all ages got the right to vote.

Returning to the examples of antiwar groups, in all, these groups signal with their names their strategies of drawing on gender norms in unconventional ways to achieve an end to war. Kutz-Flamenbaum notes that in adopting these gendered names, the groups draw on a gendered strategy for change. She writes:

... These groups challenge the assumption that war is gender neutral and that anti-war organizing should, therefore, seek to be gender neutral. In organizing as women, these groups draw attention to the differential impact of war on women, challenge gender norms by explicitly and implicitly critiquing the relationship between militarism and patriarchy, and attract media attention that, in turn, has helped integrate gender into popular representations of the anti-war movement. (2007: 90)

While Kutz-Flamenbaum focuses on performance as a gender strategy, Nancy Whittier (2001) argues that lived experiences around gender shape strategies. In her study of the predominately female movement against child sexual abuse, activists use emotional strategies shaped by their histories of abuse to "come out." She finds that adult survivors drew overtly on their emotions and did emotional labor within the movement as well as outside of it. "Activists view emotional expression as a way of breaking the silence and secrecy that characterize child sexual abuse, of releasing the emotions they were not allowed to express as children, and of learning to trust their own feelings after having been told to deny those feelings following abuse" (2001: 236). The emotional strategies of coming out as a survivor of abuse vary by context. In public demonstrations, activists may exhibit emotions of trauma around their experiences and/or resistance and pride for surviving them. In the context of talk shows, activists did the emotional labor of exhibiting aspects of pain such as sadness, fear, and vulnerability. When dealing with the state and policy makers, activists instead focused on emotions of grief, loss, and fear to establish how they had been injured, setting aside emotions such as pride and anger. They do so to respond to a political context that values rationality. "Rationality or lack of affect is a strategy of emotional display that not surprisingly is strategically useful in state institutions" (2001: 246). What Whittier documents here is – in addition to the gendered nature of strategies and emotions – how a single strategy can shift to accommodate different contexts activists find themselves in.

In sum, these examples illustrate how strategies can develop from the gender norms embedded in the sites of collective action, be specifically created in the naming and character of organizations, and/or can employ gendered emotions in the struggle for social change. Overall, in gendered societies, gendered strategies emerge as a plan to make social change. Tactics then are the actions that are employed to make that change.

Gendered Tactics

Tactics are the intentional actions that develop from the movement's or group's activist identity. They are the "novel, dramatic, unorthodox, and noninstitutional forms of political expression [that] try and shape public opinion and put pressure on those in positions of authority" (Taylor and Van Dyke 2004: 263). Tactics can be focused on public space and can work to disrupt the normal course of events through demonstrations, strikes, and marches, to performances and street theater focused on the bystander. Tactics are also used in private spaces with the writing of letters to politicians, or the decision to boycott certain foods in the grocery store, as well as the privacy of the voting booth. Movements often have multiple tactics associated with the overall strategy. Verta Taylor and Nella Van Dyke (2004) call these "tactical repertoires" or collections of tactics. For example, in the Wheeling-Pittsburgh Steel strike that opened this chapter, the strategy was to win concessions from the union through a work stoppage, the tactical repertoire included picketing, participating in community events, staffing a community kitchen and food bank, and fundraising to support the striking workers.

Social movement scholars see tactics as emerging from two main factors (Coe and Sandberg 2019). The first are structural factors that shape a movement's ability to create a tactic. Movement actors are seen as making rational decisions about their resources and pre-existing tactics when selecting the actions that they will pursue. In the Wheeling-Pittsburgh Steel strike, Humienny drew on her pre-existing relations with the community to start a food bank as one of the tactics supporting the striking workers. In another example, in the case of Take Back the Night marches, organizers said that using a routine tactic (marching) in an urban setting was an appropriate tactic when considering resources and opportunities (Coe and Sandberg 2019). If the goal of Take Back the Night is to "take back the streets" for women, a march through an area of potential danger is an appropriate tactic and one that needs few resources to accomplish.

A second set of factors comes from the identities of the activists and how the tactic aligns with how they perceive themselves. In this line of thinking, direct action (i.e. strikes and demonstrations) would come from more radical groups, less direct action (i.e. letter writing and lobbying) would come from more institutionalized groups. However, scholars argue that gender also plays a strong role in the development of tactics. I turn to the example of the March of Empty Pots as an example of how gender shapes social movement tactics.

SANTIAGO – The rhythmic pounding of empty pots and pans by thousands of Chilean women last week had the sound of war drums. In the most violent political demonstrations since President Salvador Allende Gossens took office 13 months ago, the opposition Christian Democratic and National parties took to the streets in a protest march by women and students. The incident left more than 100 persons injured, several with gunshot wounds.

The "March of the Empty Pots" last Wednesday, in which more than 5,000 women brandishing kitchenware participated, was initially a protest against food shortages. However, it blossomed into a full-fledged condemnation of Chile's left-wing Government and the activities here of Prime Minister Fidel Castro of Cuba, who ended a 25-day visit yesterday.

New York Times archives from December 5, 1971
"The World" by Juan de Onis

The Chilean Marches of the Empty Pots occurred in 1971 against Allende and again in 1983 against Pinochet and is credited with helping bring down two governments, the first, a president that struggled to get the economy under control and the second, a dictatorship. Food shortages brought on by the government (in one case mismanagement and the other an attempt to control the population) sparked the tactic of banging pots as protest and this tactic was folded into an overall strategy aimed at overthrowing the government. As discussed in Chapter 1, this was during what Rita Noonan labels the "maternal frame" period of the Chilean women's movement. A coalition of middle and upper-class women drew on their identities as mothers and engaged in more subversive protests, becoming a primary voice against the repressive Pinochet regime. Adding to the gender connotations of protest – the empty pot in the hands of a woman – is the way in which women are viewed in this culture. At this period of time, Chilean women were seen through the lens of their family roles and consequently, as political outsiders. Women's outsider status and the use of items that traditionally are associated with women illustrates how the March of the Empty Pots drew on gendered actions in an overall strategy to overthrow the government.

Indeed, social movement tactics are seldom gender neutral, even if the strategy – the overall plan – is not gendered. For example, in the case of Chile, the strategy of overthrowing the government may have been fueled by men and did not focus specifically on gender, yet the March of Empty Pots was a gendered tactic within the strategy. "Protest activity can therefore be gendered even if the intended outcomes of the activity do not center on gender issues in any direct or obvious [manner]" (Einwohner et al. 2000: 686). Scholars Anna-Britt Coe and Linda Sandberg who study feminist Take Back the Night marches in Sweden agree. They argue "gender beliefs shape tactical choices among all social movements, even those that do not aim to challenge gender inequalities" (2019: 5).

If we consider how gender is a process shaping people's lives, we can see how men and women often draw on their own "emotional responses, patterned behaviours, intellectual assertions, and reasoned decisions" (Sugiman 1992: 3) in creating tactics. In the opening scenario, we can see how Humienny drew on her socialization as a caregiver in her efforts to feed and support the striking steel workers.

Because gender also shapes society as well as individuals, men and women have different access to some tactics. Burning a draft card to protest a war has more meaning when it is done by men (who are drafted) versus women, who were not a part of a draft. However, women can draw on the status of mother in the creation of tactics which can have more resonance than men drawing on the status of father or other family roles. To explore the gender binary's influence on tactics, I first examine how traditional ideas of femininity and masculinity are a part of gendered tactics and then discuss how these norms can be transgressed.

Womanhood, femininity, and tactics

Tactically, movements have used traditional femininity by drawing on notions of motherhood and presenting conventional feminine appearances to make change. However, women can transgress gender norms as a way of making change. Anti-war groups Raging Grannies, Code Pink, and The Missile Dick Chicks provide examples of both, the use of conventional gender norms and the transgression of them. However, their gendered tactics go beyond their names. For example, in one protest Raging Grannies entered a military recruiting station armed with tea and cookies and proceeded to interact with the recruiter while other "grannies" protested outside. The group Code Pink wears pink clothing to bring a sense of unity to the members, while making them visible at anti-war demonstrations. The Missile Dick Chicks sing and dance while wearing penises and mocking elite hyper or over emphasized femininity. As illustrated by the Missile Dick Chicks, tactics can also engage the body in gendered ways. For instance, Taylor and Van Dyke (2004) note that women anti-war activists spelled out the word "peace" with their naked bodies on a beach in West Marin, California to protest the Iraq war.

However, these are by no means the only examples of women using their bodies as a gendered protest. Women have often placed themselves in front of armed police or security forces to serve as a buffer for other demonstrators. One iconic image of this tactic emerged from the Black Lives Matter movement in 2016 when Leisha Evans, a young woman clothed in summer dress and ballet flats stood immobile in front of riot-gear clad police. The image of the police rushing toward her as she stood calmly in front of them went viral as a statement of resisting police brutality. This image of forceful masculinity menacing a resisting woman breaks conventional gender norms that men are to protect women and women are to be protected from violence.

Which gendered tactics are used – conventional or transgressive – is often the result of the political environment. For example, the Irish women's movement efforts to legalize abortion often drew on conventional ideas of women, mothers, and family. Using political theater, activists boarded a ferry, creating an "abortion boat," representing the journey women take to access reproductive health services. Judy Taylor described the political theater of the trip, writing:

> The involvement of children and the use of singing; beautifully painted, colorful banners; and purple balloons further "feminized" their political action. Had women adopted more confrontational approaches to protest, customs officials might have felt more comfortable confiscating the pamphlets or roughing up and arresting those who carried them. Therefore, a great deal of feminists' tactical presentation work involved maintaining control of their political actions and safely challenging the status quo. (1998: 685)

In another example, in the #BlackLivesMatter protests of the summer of 2020, a "Wall of Moms" at the Portland, Oregon protests went viral when the "moms" lined the street in an attempt to protect other protestors (see the discussion in Chapters 2 and 3). Organized by Teressa Raiford, a Black mother and executive director of Don't Shoot Portland, the "wall" "drew mostly white moms" in the predominantly white city. Raiford, along with many observers, found that the attention the white moms received was positive as a tactic bringing attention to the protests and dismaying in its illustration of racism and white privilege. Raiford is quoted as saying, "What it does show us is that Black lives don't matter here, white moms do. And these moms know that, too. That's why they're standing in solidarity with us" (quoted in Taub 2020). When the moms were tear-gassed and beaten by the police, it incensed those seeing it and inspired a "Wall of Dads" to attend protests. The dads stood in front of the moms, many of them wearing bike helmets for protection and carrying leaf blowers to return the tear gas to the police.

While the tactics of the "abortion boat" and the "Wall of Moms" aligned with traditional ideas of femininity, movements can also violate gender norms as a tactic. In the 1960s and 1970s, young radical feminists deliberately violated gender norms of traditional femininity by not shaving their body hair, refusing to wear bras and confining girdles, and letting their hair grow long and looking "unkempt." By refusing to abide by the feminine appearance norms of the day, these feminists used their bodies as tactics to make a political statement. In a study of twenty-first-century young feminists, I found that young women and men used recycled fashion as a statement against a consumer culture that targets women. In content analysis of a feminist magazine's reoccurring fashion section, I found multiple instances of individuals combining inexpensive thrift store finds with ethnic or cultural artifacts and hand-crafted jewelry as a statement against the consumption of gendered fashion trends (2012a).

Take Back the Night (TBTN) marches, a tactic to draw attention to violence against women, seek to remake gender norms, particularly around safety and access to public spaces. The marches originate from women's inability to walk alone in urban settings at night and illustrate how fear and violence can become normalized in society, even in seemingly safe cities. Marchers then make a claim for safe space by walking through the streets, reclaiming the right to be present. "The TBTN march, as it refused normalized fear and violence in the seemingly safe city, offered a means to reclaim spaces by women and trans [people] collectively participating in city streets at night unabashedly" (Coe and Sandberg 2019: 14).

Gendered tactics also draw on other social categories. As noted, the "Wall of Moms" at the #BlackLivesMatter protests drew on traditional gender identities as well as racial identities. Social movements also use tactics that intertwine sexuality and gender. For example, Anya Galli (2016) describes how LGBTQ+ activists drew on "glitter bombing" as a short-lived tactic used to annoy their targets and gain media attention for their issues. Galli describes an incident of "glitter bombing," writing:

> In May 2011, activist Nick Espinosa waited in line at a Minneapolis book signing, hosted by openly antigay Republican presidential candidate Newt Gingrich, with a Cheez-it cracker box full of multicolored glitter tucked inside his messenger bag. In widely distributed YouTube footage of the event, Espinosa shakes hands with Gingrich and grins at the camera as he waits for the politician to sign his book. Pausing to reach into his bag and open the flaps of the box, he shakes its contents into the air over the table where Gingrich and his wife are sitting, showering them with glitter and shouting, "Feel the rainbow, Newt! Stop the hate! Stop antigay politics!" (2016: 259)

While the goal of the tactic is to draw media attention to conservative politician's anti-gay stances, "glitter bombing" also is a form of gender and sexuality transgressing where the anti-gay target is decorated in a bit of femininity and flamboyance. Just as activists draw on femininity norms; so too did they incorporate masculinity into tactics.

Manhood, masculinity, and tactics

Conventional ideas of masculinity can also be the foundation of tactics. In the Wheeling-Pittsburgh Steel strike, elements of masculinity were incorporated into the strikers' tactics. At a community parade, male workers dressed in black leather with chains and rode motorcycles to assert an image of aggressive masculinity to the community. This kind of masculinity as a tactic is also evident in some contemporary organized hate movements through the display of tattoos, shaved heads, and combat boots (Blee 2003). This tough masculinity is also evident in the genre of White Power music (Corte and Edwards 2008). White supremist organizations often use aggressive, loud and distorted rock music to draw in young men. The lyrics focus on themes about an embattled ethnic white population, promote pride in a white identity and hatred and racism toward other groups, including hostility toward any form of "race-mixing" as defined by the movement.

While this promotes a traditional and hegemonic view of masculinity, another tactic is to push men into action by noting they are *failing* at masculinity. Returning to the protests against Chilean President Allende that include the March of Empty Pots, to protest against the economic situation that left the country hungry, women repeatedly embarrassed soldiers and military officials by throwing grain at them, signifying the men as too "chicken" to fight for a change. Other movement tactics draw on traditional masculinity to convert a man's "undesired" and unmasculine identity. Lynne Gerber's study of the ex-gay movement (2015) investigates how a "godly masculinity" is constructed through a series of tactics emphasizing how men should behave. The ex-gay movement is made up of community-based ministries, regional and national organizations, therapists, pastoral counselors, congregations, and evangelical academics, and is focused on changing an individual's sexual orientation through therapy and religion. The goal is to create a "godly masculinity" that differs from hegemonic or dominant masculinity. Godly masculinity values sexual restraint and is open to a range of masculine expressions, including intimate (though not sexual) relationships with other men. These tactics frame homosexuality as a gender identity disorder and promote a heterosexual-focused masculinity (Robinson and Spivey 2007). Here traditional masculinity is used to address the "disorder" of homosexuality and includes such actions as playing sports, learning how to change a car's oil, and remembering to not cross one's legs when sitting. Godly masculinity is meant to address the erosion of masculinity brought about by gay rights and feminism and infuse masculinity with Christianity as a "vital social good" (Robinson and Spivey 2007: 668).

Movements can also transgress gender norms to make political statements. Returning to Missile Dick Chicks (Kutz-Flamenbaum 2007), we can see how women draw on aspects of masculinity in tactics. In their street theater, the Missile Dick Chicks draw on masculinity with their red, white, and blue costumes with "missile dicks" extending from their groins to create a satire linking war and masculinity. In choreographed dances and in character, the activists sing and do street theater. Kutz-Flamenbaum describes them as:

They confound their audiences by presenting themselves as stereotypically rich, conservative housewives who are drug-using, greedy, and sexually explicit and costumed like chorus girls in a jingoistic review. Militarism and masculinity are blatantly connected with the "missile dicks" incongruously attached between the legs of their red, white, and blue costumes. The clever costuming serves both to assert that men are invested in war because it affirms their masculinity and increases their profits, while viciously satirizing women who are invested in defending the militaristic and capitalist status quo because it protects their luxurious lifestyle. (2007: 98–99)

Gendered transgressive performances can also be used as a form of protest. For example, drag shows can be seen as part of the tactical repertoire of the gay and lesbian movement (Taylor, Rupp, and Gamson 2004). Called "entertaining collective events in which cross-dressing is used to call attention to the role of cultural markers and practices such as dress, bodily style, gesture and voice, in constructing gender and sexual difference" (2004: 107). Gay male drag queens "contest dominant heterosexual gender codes" in their performances, drawing on the body as a protest tactic (2004: 111). In a study of the 801 Cabaret in Key West, Verta Taylor, Leila Rupp, and Joshua Gamson found that drag queens intentionally shaped performances that disrupted gender and that audience members, despite coming for entertainment only, found themselves discussing gender "disturbances" and sexual and gender diversity after viewing the performances.

While movements develop gendered tactics that activists use to achieve their desired outcomes; they also draw on tactics from other movements in a process called social movement spillover (Meyer and Whittier 1994). For example, tactics created in the women's movement were adopted later in the peace movement. The spillover of one movement's tactics to another is common throughout history and that spillover often brings with it gendered dynamics. David Meyer and Nancy Whittier argue that the women's movement of the 1960s and 1970s shaped the peace movement in the 1980s, in part, through the use of gendered tactics. They write:

Many actions by women's peace groups drew on a feminist tradition of theatrical tactics dramatizing the feminist frame linking militarism to patriarchy. For example, in 1981 and 1982 the Women's Pentagon Action staged large demonstrations and civil disobedience actions outside the Pentagon, linking the nuclear arms race to broader social injustices, including violence against women, poverty, and other violations of human rights. The Pentagon actions included expressions of mourning for societal injustice, anger at the perpetrators of injustice, and ended with participants symbolically "exorcising" the evil spirits of the Pentagon by weaving a "web of life" around the building, simultaneously trying to shut the building down. These symbols reprised decades-old self-consciously dramatic tactics. Activists combined direct political action with spiritual rituals they claimed drew on the strength of goddesses and other sources of women's power. The effects of these events spread beyond the hundreds of women who participated, as the activists took the tactics and inspiration back to local communities where they organized a wide variety of campaigns. (1994: 287–288)

"Hidden" Gendered Strategies and Tactics

Despite the ease in which gender intertwines with tactics and strategies, the gendered nature of some can cause them to be missed (Staggenborg and Taylor 2005). For example, while some may see runs and walkathons to address breast cancer as apolitical and focused in the realm of self-help, there are distinct movement strategies and tactics at play. In Maren Klawiter's study of three breast cancer campaigns, she finds that some campaigns draw on heteronormative and heterosexual femininity (1999). For example, in her observations of the Race for the Cure, the focus was on the importance of biomedicine with considerable attention to beauty and fashion services including a marketplace showcasing a range of breast prostheses for different activities, wigs and scarves to hide the results of chemotherapy, and pink visors for the survivors of breast cancer. The other breast cancer walks – Women and Cancer Walk and Toxic Tour – did not focus on the creation of "appropriate" feminine appearances and beauty and instead focused on social justice and the surrounding community. For instance, the Women and Cancer walk had women who purposively did not hide their loss of breasts or hair as a result of cancer, challenging norms of beauty, womanhood, and femininity. What Klawiter reveals in her study is the way in which a traditional view of femininity is embedded in the tactic of some breast cancer walks, only made obvious through comparisons to other walks. While the goal is to end breast cancer, the submerged gendering of the tactic can hide its political intent.

In a related example, feminists in the 1960s and 1970s worked to undo the relationship between femininity, womanhood, and activities such as parenting, and homemaking, while critiquing feminine activities such as beauty and make-up routines and fashion. In an attempt to recast some of these feminine activities as worthwhile, twenty-first-century feminists have focused on reclaiming "disparaged girl things" such as fashion, make-up, and crafting that they feel was discarded and marginalized by earlier feminists. Scholars have examined this reclaiming of gendered activities such as knitting, quilting, sewing, and crafting as political. For example, knitting "guru" Debbie Stoller is quoted as saying, "valuing the craft of knitting is a feminist act in itself . . . because the denigration of knitting correlates directly with the denigration of traditionally women-centred activity" (Pentney 2008: 1). In addition, some twenty-first-century feminist knitting communities can be seen as a gendered form of activism that can shape alternative understandings of masculinity and femininity, particularly when people of all genders come together (Kelly 2014, 2015). These are examples of activities that are often not seen as political but when done within the context of a movement and infused with ideas of gender, they are tactics of everyday activism.

In addition, gendered tactics can be submerged in "unobtrusive" settings. Mary Katzenstein's study of the Catholic Church and the armed services (1990) illustrates how activism to change the institutions was done by insiders. While the two institutions varied in terms of culture, women activists worked within them to bring changes to each. Katzenstein writes, "Operating outside the arena of conventional politics or social organizing, groups of women have established a presence in the constituent institutions of the American state and of society" (1990: 53).

While some tactics and strategies are missed because of the way in which womanhood or femininity is incorporated in them, there is another missing element. Masculinity has been largely ignored in the analysis of tactics and strategies. This is primarily the result of viewing men as the norm and therefore not gendered and viewing men as the default, that is "expected" activists. Women and their actions are often the focus of researchers and the public when they become visible in ways that do not align with traditional gender ideologies. The idea that women and femininity do not traditionally equal activist and activism has led to a greater scrutiny of women and women's movements than the actions of men and masculinity. Taking a gendered lens to social movements with a focus on masculinity is needed to have a complete view of how gender shapes social change.

Conclusion

In sum, gender as a sorting mechanism provides us with social locations and access to power is evident in the internal workings of social movements. This is particularly true in the looking at leadership. Although the histories of social movements are filled with men as leaders, women were (and are) leaders but often in ways that are not acknowledged by the organizations they are in. Cecelia Humienny in the Wheeling-Pittsburgh Steelworkers' strike is an example of a woman shut out of some forms of leadership by the men around her, who found a way to lead despite them.

The participants in movements draw on stereotypes and gender assumptions about leadership and those ideas and gender norms can shape the way women can do leadership. Even leaderless protests such as Occupy have leaders, and research illustrates how – even in a more contemporary movement – women, genderqueer and people of color face harassment, derision, and sexual assault when they assume leadership roles (Hurwitz 2019).

These ideas about gender also shape the strategies and tactics that movements adopt. Some movements adopt strategies and tactics that align with societal views of gender, particularly femininity. However, movements may purposely transgress and violate gender norms in their strategies and tactics. Movement histories are filled with the ways in which women have transgressed norms of femininity in their work for peace, anti-war, suffrage, liberation, and other movements.

Yet, despite the use of gender in some movement strategies and tactics, some gendered meanings remain submerged and hidden. Judith Lorber (1990) reminds us that for people thinking about gender is like a fish thinking about water – it is simply all around and is often unidentifiable. I now turn to what happens when movements do focus on gender and shift gender norms and conceptions. As a result, some groups in society gain new ways of claiming a gender identity and others work to resist and retain traditional gender ideas.

Sources to Explore

Crawford, Vicki L., Jacqueline Anne Rouse, and Barbara Woods (eds.). 1990. *Women in the civil rights movement: Trailblazers and torchbearers, 1941–1965.* Bloomington, IN: Indiana University Press.

Kretschmer, Kelsy. https://theconversation.com/video-the-wall-of-moms-builds-on-a-long-protest-tradition-143958

Schneider, Nathan. 2012. Some assembly required: Witnessing the birth of Occupy Wall Street. *Harpers*, February. https://www.nonviolent-conflict.org/wp-content/uploads/2016/01/schneider_some_assembly_required.pdf

Women and the civil rights movement. https://www.nps.gov/articles/women-and-the-civil-rights-movement.htm

Podcast on the March of Empty Pots. https://www.forgingmemory.org/narrative/march-empty-pots-and-pans

Questions to Consider

1. What makes someone a leader? How is gender a part of that characterization and how do feminist scholars challenge that characterization?
2. Can you describe the difference between a tactic and strategy and provide an example of each?
3. How are traditional femininity and gender norms for women incorporated into social movement tactics and strategies?
4. How is traditional masculinity incorporated into social movement tactics and strategies? How is masculinity transgressed?
5. What are some ways that activists can use gender transgression in their tactics? Can you think of other examples of gender transgression in other areas of social life?

Reflection

Thinking about men as "default" activists, how is the invisibility of masculinity evident in other areas of social life?

5

Legacies of Rise and Resistance: How Gender Sparks Change and Backlash

The April 8th 2013 covers of *TIME* Magazine.
Credit: Esther Vargas/Flickr

It is the fall of 1987 and hundreds of thousands of gay men, lesbians, and allies gather at the 2nd National March on Washington for Lesbian and Gay Rights. In front of the Internal Revenue Service Building the protestors stopped, blocking the street. Couples turned to each other and, led by the organization Couples Inc., took part in a collective wedding. As they vowed to love and honor each other, their protest, as a form of street theater, was meant to draw attention to the legalized discrimination lesbian and gay couples face. Couples Inc. released a statement of their demands which included the statement: "Recognizing and celebrating the diversity in family relationships, we demand legal recognition of lesbian and gay male domestic partnerships with all the benefits and entitlements that flow from marriage."

March on Washington (1987)

States cannot keep same-sex couples from marrying and must recognize their unions, the Supreme Court says in a ruling that for months has been the focus of speculation. The decision was 5–4. Justice Anthony Kennedy, seen as a pivotal swing vote in the case, wrote the majority opinion. All four justices who voted against the ruling wrote their own dissenting opinions: Chief Justice John Roberts and Justices Antonin Scalia, Clarence Thomas and Samuel Alito.

"They ask for equal dignity in the eyes of the law," Kennedy wrote of same-sex couples in the case. "The Constitution grants them that right." ... The Supreme Court said that the right to marry is fundamental – and Kennedy wrote that under the 14th Amendment's protections, "couples of the same sex may not be deprived of that right and that liberty."

"Supreme Court Declares Same-Sex Marriage Legal in All 50 States"
Bill Chappell, National Public Radio (June 26, 2015)

So far in our discussion of gender and social movements, we have examined these fundamental questions – How does gender shape the movements people form and how do they come to and act in movements? How does gender shape the dynamics and pathways of movements? In this chapter, I take a different approach and ask how can ideas of gender shape a movement and how do social movements change gender? To address the question of how ideas of gender can shape movements, I begin with two scenarios from LGBTQ+ movement around same-sex marriage. While these scenarios of street theater weddings and a Supreme Court decision appear to be solely about sexuality and sexual identity, they also addressed core issues of gender. The goals of the 1987 March on Washington and the activist work that resulted in the 2015 Supreme Court decision legalizing same-sex marriage included expanding gendered notions of the family and normalizing LGBTQ+ families. This gendered remaking of the family was accomplished in many ways, including the dissemination of images of LGBTQ+ families in campaigns with slogans like "Love makes a family" as well as legislative efforts to undo gendered and heteronormative stereotypes in adoption, custody, and other family-related cases.

While all of this seems like progress for LGBTQ+ people, some argue that remaking the gay family as equivalent to heterosexual families ignores the radical potential of LGBTQ+ people to change society and undo notions of gender and sexual identity. Scholar Suzanna Danuta Walters in her analysis of tolerance of queer people in society versus integration asks, "How might full inclusion undermine the sexist masculinity at the heart of military culture? What can queer kinship say to nuclear families?" (2014: 259). In doing so, she points to the ways in which traditional heterosexual gender norms have been incorporated into some of the mainstream LGBTQ+ movements' efforts. She goes on to note that "The default zone of heterosexual nuclear family life goes unquestioned here, and in the process, possibilities for thinking outside the hetero box get narrowed even further" (2014: 260).

The disjunction between the celebration of the right to same-sex marriage and the criticism of it as a form of gender and sexual assimilation, illustrates how conceptions of gender shape desired movement outcomes and how those conceptions are debated within movements. To some activists, the right to marry asserts their similarity to heterosexual society, while for other activists identifying as queer has the radical potential to undo how gender, sex, and sexuality sort society. It also illustrates a core dynamic about social movements in general examined throughout this book – social movements are rarely made up of people who all agree on the end goal. When a particular outcome is sought, there are multiple outcomes – some groups get what they want, others are left out and some don't agree with the direction of change. Others in society actively work to oppose change. I begin this chapter by exploring this dynamic – how as ideas about gender are changed by movements – changing ideas of gender also influence movements. In particular, I focus on how transgender and gender non-binary people break down the gender binary; while they have often struggled to be a part of contemporary social movements.

Breaking Down the Binary

Much of the research in this book on social movements and gender understand gender as a binary where either men or women (occasionally both sexes) are examined in social movements. These studies examine cisgender individuals whose personal identity and gender corresponds with the sex identified for them at birth. Yet, gender is more fluid than a binary with identities that include transgender, genderqueer, gender fluid, and gender non-conforming people among other identities. In addition, some people identify as agender, that is, having no gender identity at all. Scholar Susan Stryker defines transgender as those "who move away from the gender they were assigned at birth, people who cross over (*trans-*) the boundaries constructed by their culture to define and contain that gender" (2017: 1). Scholar Ann Travers adopts a similar definition noting that transgender refers to "people who defy societal expectations of gender" (2018: 2). Both Stryker and Travers note that not all people who defy the gender binary identify as transgender and that "the widest imaginable array of gender-variant practices and identities" should be included in societal understandings (Stryker 2017: 38). In sum, transgender is "… a very complex term that alludes to an identity, a set of transgressions to gender, a critical lens to think through gender normativity, and even masculinity and femininity themselves" (Vidal-Ortiz 2020: 466). Overall, the notion of "trans" in transgender, has the potential to undo all binaries and reconstruct how gender, sex, and sexuality are understood. Through trans, those understandings are constantly shifted and redefined.

While for some in society these might seem like new ways of thinking and doing gender, transgender and non-confirming individuals have always been a part of society, whether they were acknowledged or not (Feinberg 1996; Stryker 2017). At the end of the twentieth century, sociologist Betsy Lucal wrote about her own conflicting experiences of not fitting in the binary in her autoethnography. Lucal, who did not strike an overtly feminine appearance but did not intentionally seek to look masculine, reflected on what it is like to live ricocheting back and forth in the gender binary. She noted, "I am, in effect, both woman and not-woman. As a woman who is often a social man but who also is a woman living in a patriarchal society, I am in a unique position to see and act. I sometimes receive privileges limited to men, and I sometimes am oppressed by my status as a deviant woman" (1999: 793). Lucal's analysis of her relationship to the gender binary serves as a reminder of how "doing gender" (West and Zimmerman 1987) has long been complicated for many people.

Writer Leslie Feinberg in a history of transgender people notes that gender diversity has always existed and gender "has been expressed differently in diverse historical periods, cultures, regions, nationalities, and classes" (1996: 121). While transgender people have always existed in society, the term "transgender" is thought to have originated somewhere between the 1960s and the 1980s and came into popular usage in the 1990s (Weiss 2009; Stryker 2017). Since the 1990s, societal attention to transgender has multiplied exponentially with coverage in mainstream magazines such as *National Geographic* and *Time* magazine, and the portrayal of trans characters in movies and TV, and trans-based reality TV shows. Just as mainstream society has focused on issues of transgender and gender expression, so too have social movements. Feinberg connects the history of trans people to one of working for social change, writing "As trans people, we have a history of resistance of which we should be proud. We have stood up to the slave-owners, the feudal landlords, and the capitalist bosses" (1996: 128). To explore the connection between trans, transgender people and social movements, I examine two movements: the U.S. women's movement and the U.S. LGBTQ+ movement and conclude by discussing the rise of a separate transgender movement.

Transgender and feminism

The U.S. women's movement responded to transgender people, particularly trans women, in two distinct ways – exclusion and denial on one hand and inclusion and acceptance on the other. Despite the core ideology of feminism to undo the disadvantages of gender inequality, these two responses take very different paths. One outcome of feminists' attention to gender is that masculinity and femininity are seen as fluid and not strictly aligned to sex categories. Just as the lesbian and gay men did street theater weddings to protest the privileged ideal of the heterosexual family, many feminists worked to undo the connection of sex (male and female) with gender (woman or man), undoing essentialist gender stereotypes. The articulation of intersectionality further complicated what it meant to be a woman and moved some feminists away from the belief in the "universal" woman (i.e. conceived of as a white, middle-class woman). Instead intersectional feminists argue that to understand a woman's life, one must consider all the aspects of that life including race, class, sexuality, and gender expression among others.

This idea of challenging gender inequality, and consequently the gender binary, made feminism a place where some trans women found an activist home. As noted by scholar Miriam Abelson, "As long as there have been transgender people and feminist movements, there have been trans people active in them" (2019: 43). In her analysis of transgender and feminism, Abelson found that many transmasculine people continued to identify with feminism, endorsing the notion that there many feminisms, and no one group represented all feminists. This allowed them to focus on the cisgender feminists who were accepting and inclusive of trans people.

However, there is also a long, documented history of trans exclusion by feminists, particularly radical feminists who were more likely to see men and women as essentially (i.e. biologically) different and that trans women were not "truly" women. These feminists, adopting the slogan "The personal is political," were critical of the individual practices of trans women to alter their bodies in any way. These practices were perceived as personal solutions to societal problems, doing nothing to eradicate the structures that maintain gender inequality (Stryker 2017). This resulted in a period in the 1970s of feminist transphobia in the movement that Stryker labels "a perfect storm of hostility toward transgender issues" (2017: 127). The decade brought numerous attacks on trans women who sought to be involved in feminism. Trans women were told that they were not "real" women since they had not lived their entire lives as women and that their gender transitions reinforced harmful gender stereotypes. One of the key proponents of that ideology is Janice Raymond who authored a book entitled, *The transsexual empire: The making of the she-male.* In the book, Raymond equates transsexuality with the rape of women's bodies, and claims that transsexuals bring patriarchal oppression to women, linking them with Nazi experimentation (Stryker 2017).

While Raymond's views on transgender are extreme, and are ones she continues to hold, transphobia was evident in other feminist communities. One of the most prominent examples of this is the exclusion of trans women from the Michigan Womyn's Music Festival held yearly in the U.S. from 1976 to 2015. The festival drew thousands of women each year from around the globe for a week of camping and open-air concerts. The festival organizers had a policy that only women-born-women and girls should be allowed in, along with boys under the age of four. In 1991, a trans woman was expelled from the festival. In 1994, as a result of the policy and the expulsion, transgender activists protested, setting up Camp Trans, across from the festival site. This standoff between the festival and Camp Trans continued until 2015, when the festival shut down. While the Michigan Womyn's Music Festival had a specific policy on trans women, other feminist spaces could also be exclusive, even without a set policy.

In late 1990s, issues of trans exclusion also arose with the performances of the *Vagina Monologues,* a series of performance pieces written by Eve Ensler that focus on women's physical, sexual, and health-related experiences with their vaginas. Based on interviews with cis women, the monologues became a mainstay on college campuses, raising money for a series of causes. As quickly as performances of the monologues spread, concerns about the essentialist use of the vagina to represent womanhood were raised, leading many to call the monologues transphobic and damaging to intersex people. Debates about whether the monologues were either empowering or disparaging raged on college campuses, with many rewriting the monologues to be more inclusive and sensitive to the portrayals of non-Western, indigenous, and trans women. For example in 2015, the women's college Mount Holyoke decided to stop performing the monologues after doing so for decades after the college redefined its definition of "woman" to include transgender students. "Many felt the play was neither inclusive nor representative of the student body" (Edwards 2015: online).

Overall, trans women have struggled to find acceptance within feminist spaces. Sally Hines (2005) interviewed British trans women and men on their experiences in feminist community events and spaces and found that many felt rejected, particularly in spaces organized by radical feminists. This was particularly true for trans men who had been active in feminism and now felt excluded after their transition. However, many of Hines' interviewees found contemporary feminist and queer spaces more open and accepting than ones from previous generations.

Despite more openness than before, cis feminists still struggle with transgender issues, despite large numbers of younger feminists who support transgender rights. Some feminist organizations and websites still endorse the exclusion of transgender people and have been labeled as TERFs, trans-exclusionary radical feminists. Organizations such as the Women's Liberation Front or WoLF and Hands Across the Aisle have actively worked to stop court cases advocating trans rights. WoLF describes themselves as "A women-only organization: We are females who survived girlhood" and seeks the abolishing of gender altogether (WoLF no date). Other communities of cis feminists see no boundaries based on gender identities and welcome and support trans people. A young feminist in a community in the northeast United States said, "I think that definitely transgender people are a part of the feminist movement because I just think that [the] feminist movement [is] standing up and doing something about being discriminated against" (Reger 2012: 174). Indeed, Abelson (2019) concludes that even when cisgender feminists have not had the loudest voices in these debates, transfeminism exists and offers all feminists new possibilities for social change. In sum, the history of trans people and feminism is a complicated one with places and times of great marginalization and discrimination, and other places and times of acceptance and inclusion.

LGBTQ+ movement and transgender

Just as aspects of feminism pushed against the gender binary, so did the LGBTQ+ movement with transgender being incorporated as the "T." The movement, in all its historical iterations, started with the struggle for the fundamental right to exist, and developed into a more complex questioning of heterosexual society and sexuality as a binary. As the movement opened new identities and ideas around gender, sex, and sexuality, it also created space for the articulation of identities outside the sexuality binary.

However just as with U.S. feminism, the history of trans people within the LGBTQ+ movement is one of inclusion at times, and marginalization and exclusion at others. Some of the most important actions of the modern movement have their roots in the actions of drag queens, who may not have identified as transgender, but definitely could be characterized as gender rebels.

Keeping in mind that in the 1950s and 1960s it was illegal to dress in the "opposite" sex clothing in public, drag queens were often the targets of police harassment and the first to fight back. While the 1969 Stonewall Riot in New York City is the most well-known action, with drag queens leading the resistance against police harassment, historians argue that drag queens were key in earlier protests, such as the Compton Cafeteria Riot of 1966, where drag queens and transvestites (i.e. the language of the time) fought back. Two prominent activists Marsha P. Johnson and Sylvia Rivera co-founded STAR (Street Transvestite Action Revolutionaries) after Stonewall in 1970 to help educate and protect street kids. STAR was one of several trans-focused organizations that developed in the 1970s. However pivotal their role, drag queens were often relegated to the margins of the movement. Organizers of the Christopher Street Liberation Day tried to prevent Rivera from speaking because drag queens were seen as parodying women by lesbian feminists. When she did speak, while being booed by the crowd, she criticized the gay liberation movement for its focus on white, middle-class gays and lesbians (Abelson 2019). While pioneers such as Rivera were disparaged because of their gendered dress and demeanor, the tension between many drag queens and the mainstream gay and lesbian movement is also one of racism. Salvador Vidal-Ortiz calls them "non-white pioneers" and notes that "transgender history is connected to bodies and subjects in the U.S. that were always already external to its core: José Sarria, Sylvia Rivera, and Marsha P. Johnson" (2020: 468).

Just as drag queens and trans women were key in the uprising of the modern gay liberation movement of the 1960s and were often not acknowledged, Stryker argues that trans people have always struggled to fit into the LGB movement. This is particularly true in periods when homonormativity in mainstream gay culture promoted an appearance that was "straight looking and straight acting" (Stryker 2017: 119–120). This distancing of trans people from the mainstream movement was further exacerbated when homosexuality was removed from American Psychiatric Association's Diagnostic and Statistical Manual of Mental Disorders (DSM) in 1974. As a result, one source of connection between lesbians, gay men, and trans people, the way in which they were viewed by the mental health establishment, was severed (Stryker 2017). Exacerbating this, Gender Identity Disorder, a diagnostic categorization that psychopathologizes transgender people, was added in the next edition of the DSM. The result was a lose–lose situation for transgender people, who had no choice but to be considered "bad, sick, or wrong" (Stryker 2017: 141).

This disconnect between trans rights and the mainstream movement continues. Michelle O'Brien (2019) notes that LGBTQ+

organizations lose their focus on transgender rights when outcomes sought by gender confirming, elite gay male donors are satisfied with other gains. She found that after working to successfully pass legislation in New York State in 2011 recognizing same-sex marriage, the group, Empire Pride Agenda closed down a few years later. It did so after donor support, from mostly elite, white, gay males, slowed down. O'Brien observed:

> One former board co-chair and the organization's most enthusiastic donor in support of transgender rights explained the difficulties after winning the marriage campaign: "People have said, 'I'll give you money this year, but it's the last year. That's not my issue' . . . They said 'trans people should have their rights, but that's not our issue.'" "That's not my issue," was echoed as a common donor sentiment across multiple interviews [for the study]. (2019: 595)

As a result, the organization failed to pass statewide legislation protecting trans people from discrimination. O'Brien's research illustrates how the "T" in LGBTQ+ can be excluded or ignored when it does not align with other identities in an organization.

The dismissal of trans-related concerns was also evident when Jennicet Gutiérrez, an advocate for trans Latina women, confronted President Obama at a White House reception in 2015, while he was giving a speech for pride month. Gutiérrez, an undocumented trans woman, interrupted President Obama to publicly demand that he free undocumented LGBTQ+ immigrants held in U.S. detention centers. She was removed from the reception and her statements caused a rift between "those who supported Gutiérrez – radical and progressive queers – and those who did not – mostly cisgender gay men and lesbian women whose battle for same-sex marriage seemed to take precedence over their battle for rights" (Vidal-Ortiz 2020: 464). As these incidences illustrate, the fight for rights for transgender and gender non-conforming individuals has a long history of being shunted aside when more mainstream goals are sought by LGB organizations.

Rise of the trans social justice movement

Despite serious issues of marginalization and exclusion, the women's and LGBTQ+ movements created spaces where trans people could find each other and offer mutual support. While the 1970s and 1980s were difficult times for trans people in both the women's and LGBTQ+ movements, the 1990s brought new attention to transgender issues and transgender activism in what could be labeled as the trans social justice movement.

In the United States, trans activists work for the right to change sex status on driver's licenses, to pass human and civil rights protections, and to elect transgender or trans supportive politicians. The group Transgender Nation formed in 1992 and transgender studies and queer theory spread into academia. With the advent of the internet and social media, transgender activism and organizations continue to grow. The 2000s brought transgender activism to new levels with the presidency of Barack Obama, who included transgender rights in his agenda despite criticism from activists such as Gutiérrez. This was also a time where issues of gender-neutral bathrooms arose and "penis panics" about trans women in women's restrooms emerged.[4] While some of the gains of the early 2000s period were reversed with Donald Trump's presidency, many universities and public buildings now include gender-neutral bathrooms, as well as gender-neutral fitting rooms in some clothing chains. Other accomplishments include the ability (in some places) to change gender on official ID cards and the growing discipline of trans studies in universities and colleges.

While there has been national-level activism in the trans social justice movement, there are also many organizations that work at the grassroots or community level. Heath Davis (2017) details one such organization – RAGE or Riders Against Gender Exclusion. RAGE grew out of the need to draw public attention to the ways in which transgender people face discrimination in using public transportation. The Southeastern Pennsylvania Transportation Authority (SEPTA) marked transit passes with sex indication stickers – F for female and M for male. Davis notes that passengers "whose appearance also challenged prevailing gender norms" were denied entrance onto buses or were harassed by bus operators (2017: 3). Using social media, the RAGE collected stories of abuse and discrimination and launched protests including a street theater drag show and the creation of a Rider's Bill of Rights. After years of back and forth with the SEPTA management, the sex indication sticker was removed from transit passes.

In addition, grassroots organizations such as *El/la Trans Latina* work with transgender Latina women offering services around HIV, violence prevention and leadership development with the goal of strengthening the community in the San Francisco area. In Washington D.C., the *Casa Ruby*, started by an immigrant transwoman, offers housing, healthcare, and violence prevention to LGBTQ+ people. The group *Corpora en Libertad* offers support to trans women in prisons throughout Latin America. Overall, trans social justice activism has spread around the world and focuses on a variety of issues. Trans activism includes lobbying for gender identity laws, education and employment opportunities and protections, community work, and the use of arts to establish trans identities and rights. Vidal-Ortiz sees this activism in a variety of countries including the United States, Canada, Argentina, and Mexico (2020).

These diverse types of grassroots trans activism not only benefit their communities but also can open up opportunities for the next trans generation. In her book titled *The trans generation: How trans kids (and their parents) are creating a gender revolution*, Ann Travers (2018) documents the issues and dangers trans kids and their families face. Travers concludes that there are four main tasks facing those who seek change: making space for kids to determine their own gender identities, setting up gender-affirming and accessible healthcare, dismantling gender inequality while protecting those who do not identify in the binary, and focusing on vulnerable kids and the connection to the criminal justice system and incarceration. Travers argues that doing so will create "a vision of a more just and equitable future for all of us" (2018: 201).

In sum, when considering transgender and non-conforming individuals in social movements, it is evident there is a complicated and, at times, troublesome history with lingering roots in the present. In the women's movement, the fight for gender equality is seen as essential, yet, what makes a person "a woman" continues to be debated, and trans people continue to be marginalized by some feminists. In the LGBTQ+ movement, the issues facing trans and gender non-conforming people can get lost in the struggle for rights organized more around sexuality and sexual identity versus gender and gender identity. Yet social movement scholarship tells us that when people are faced with inequality, have access to resources, and can organize themselves in some way, creating a shared identity, movements emerge. The emergence of the trans social justice movement and grassroots activism is evidence of this. I now turn to what happens when societal pressure or movements seeking to stop or reverse change arise.

Societal Backlash and the Rise of Countermovements

When movements are successful in obtaining some of their goals, they often draw the attention of the status quo and mainstream society. Because movements are oppositional, they often face a strong reaction to their goals and achievements. When multiple forces in mainstream society, such as legislative bodies, popular culture and the media, coalesce against a movement and its gains, scholars label this a societal backlash. A backlash differs from the more organized countermovement that emerges specifically to stop or reverse the gains of another movement. Across the globe, the history of social movements is one of backlash and countermovements moving to stop or reverse change. Movements that address gender norms often face fierce opposition and find some of their gains contested through backlash and countermovements. I now turn to how the history of the U.S. women's movement as an example of backlash and organized countermovement challenges.

Mainstream backlash

When movements, such as women's movements, appear to be winning some of their goals, one result is a societal backlash that ridicules the movement and participants. Sociologist Myra Marx Ferree (2004) notes that opposed to "harsh" repression that uses violence and force, this kind of repression is "soft" and seeks to mock and ridicule the movement and those who believe in it. The goal of harsh and soft repression is to silence and/or eradicate the movement altogether. The history of the U.S. women's movement is one mostly of soft repression. At various times in its history, the movement and feminists have been ridiculed to the point where to identify as a feminist or someone who believes in feminism could bring scorn, mocking, and marginalization. Feminists have been stereotyped as "man haters," "lesbians," and "humorless nags," among other negative labels (Reger 2012).

This backlash against feminism led to what I call the "everywhere and nowhere" of the women's movement (Reger 2012). These stereotypes and marginalization of the movement come from social commentators who see feminism as "nowhere," meaning no longer relevant or present in U.S. society. Feminism is often declared "dead" by social pundits and no longer relevant as a way of eradicating the movement, a move that signals the movement's strength. For instance, the 1990s were repeatedly noted as a time where young women and men were no longer interested in or needed feminism, despite evidence that feminism was embedded in communities and grassroots activism. The notion of feminism's death was challenged in 2017 when women's marches sprang up around the globe, protesting the election of Donald Trump and illustrating that feminism is in fact, "everywhere" and had not gone away.

Despite this, obituaries for feminism recur throughout the movement's history. For example, after suffragists won the right to vote in 1920, the movement was declared dead and irrelevant by the 1950s. Social commentators filled the media with notices that the movement was no longer needed and magazines and newspapers were filled with reports of happy homemakers who had no interest in feminism (Rupp and Taylor 1987). When the movement resurged in the late 1960s and early 1970s, commentators again declared the movement dead a few decades later. For instance, in 1998, *Time* magazine ran a cover story with the headline "Is Feminism Dead?" complete with pictures of Susan B. Anthony, Betty Friedan, Gloria Steinem, and TV character Ally McBeal. The author minimized the movement of the time noting, "If feminism of the '60s and '70s was steeped in research and obsessed with social change, feminism today is wed to the culture of celebrity and self-obsession" (Bellafante 1998: 25). Also in the late 1990s, when a young, punk-infused feminism, notably in Riot Grrrl, emerged in the Northwest United States, it quickly became the focus of condescending media coverage that mocked participants and brought about a media boycott by figures in the movement (Marcus 2010). These obits for feminism continued into the 2000s, drawing on a combination of silencing and ridicule. Ariel Levy (2005) argued that feminism was seen as no longer having nationally visible groups and institutionally focused goals. As a result, feminism in the 2000s was charged with being apolitical and only concerned with dress, appearance, and individualized empowerment (Levy 2005).

A decade into the 2000s, the death of feminism was still the subject of discussion with prominent media such as the *New York Times* running headlines such as "Where to pass the torch?" (Winerip 2009), or the *American Prospect*'s article titled the "The end of the women's movement" (Martin 2009). A more recent example is the 2020 opinion piece in the *New York Times* entitled "Feminism has failed women." The subhead read, "If the pandemic undid three decades of progress on gender equality, one has to wonder: How real was the progress the first place?" (Brooks 2020: online). In sum, as a movement that challenges societal structure, power, and privilege through gender, the U.S. women's movement has been declared dead or incompetent repeatedly as a strategy to divert its energy and focus (Hawkesworth 2004). However, as I noted, feminism is also "everywhere," drawing on the idea that as social movements continue over long periods of time, their ideas and goals are absorbed into culture and are per-vasive, becoming a part of everyday cultural beliefs and norms. Just as feminist authors Jennifer Baumgardner and Amy Richards (2000: 17) noted, "Feminism is like fluoride, it is simply in the water." Or, as Ednie Kaeh Garrison (2005) describes it, feminism is in the airwaves around us. So, if feminism hasn't ended and, in fact, continues – where does this backlash come from?

Susan Faludi published a best-selling book in 1991 titled, *Backlash: The undeclared war against American women.* In it she documents how advances for gender equality by the move-ment brought significant pushback from a variety of sources. She illustrates how the media, film, novels, and pop psychology damn feminism for causing women's misery and unhappiness, and notes that the government and some academics supported this idea with policies and research. For instance, she notes how the news media, in the late 1980s, began to focus on the issues faced by women in the workplace, coverage she labels "the curse of the career woman" (1991: 105). Media reports on women's lack of marriage partners, involuntary childlessness, fertility issues, flourished, all due to the change in the status owed to feminism. Faludi notes that at the same time as this backlash, women still had much to gain to achieve true equality. At the time of her writing, women represented two-thirds of poor adults, had lower incomes than men, were tracked into "female" jobs with fewer opportunities, received less financial aid than men for college, and still did a "second shift" of housework (1991), all trends that persist. Not only did proponents of the backlash ignore aspects of gender inequality, they also worked to divide women. She writes:

It [the backlash] pursues a divide-and-conquer strategy; single women versus married women, working women versus homemakers, middle- versus working-class. It manipulates a system of rewards and punishments, elevating women who follow its rules, isolating women who don't. The backlash remarkets old myths about women as new facts and ignores all appeals to reason. Cornered, it denies its own existence, points an accusatory finger at feminism, and burrows deeper underground. (1991: xxii)

Faludi's coverage of the backlash illustrates that in addressing gender, women's movements around the world seek to change "one of the most fundamental relations of power" (Staggenborg and Taylor 2005: 48). Consequently, when power starts to shift; backlash results, and countermovements can rise.

Countermovements

The Army of God assembles at 5: 30 A.M. in the Melodyland parking lot. Cars wear the bumper sticker "Be a Hero, Save a Whale; Save a Baby, Go To Jail." . . . When we arrive [at the abortion clinic], about 200 prochoicers are waiting in the front and the back of the one-story, brick building, waving blue-and-white signs that read "Keep Abortion Legal," stamping their feet on the ground as they yell, "Not the Church, not the state, women must decide their fate!" . . . The main back door has been secured by the prochoicers and about 30 rescuers are sent to sit in front of them. And so on and so on until there is a kind of club sandwich of political views – Keep Abortion Legal, then photographs of bloody fetuses, Keep Your Hands Off of My Body, then bloody fetuses, then coat hangers.

Kathy Dobie, Village Voice, April 11, 1989
(Cited by Meyer and Staggenborg 1996)

Whenever movements push for change in one direction, movements can arise that seek to stop change from happening or to erase gains from other movements. The scenario above is an example of these interactions. The struggle over abortion has been between a "pro-choice" movement for legalized abortion and accessible contraception and family planning and a "pro-life" countermovement seeking to end abortion and some forms of birth control. While the United States is the site of this movement–countermovement conflict, movement–countermovement interactions exist across the globe from Central America to Western Europe (Meyer and Staggenborg 1996). In the United States, they note that there are movement–countermovement struggles over a range of issues including gay rights, animal rights, gun control, nuclear power, and environmental policies, among others. These interactions are not unusual. "Any social movement of potential political significance will generate opposition" and that opposition comes in the form of a countermovement "that makes contrary claims simultaneously to those of the original movement" (Meyer and Staggenborg 1996: 1630, 1631). When one movement succeeds in obtaining its goals and/or a portion of the population is threatened by the movement's goal countermovements can arise. While the struggle over abortion rights has many facets, one key factor is how women's role in society is understood and what rights women have over their lives and their bodies. As we have seen, gender is a powerful organizing structure in society, and changes to gendered norms and patterns can seem threatening to portions of a population who benefit from those norms remaining unchanged. Two movements in the United States addressing gender that have sparked opposition are the suffrage movement lasting from the 1860s to 1920 and the struggle to ratify the Equal Rights Amendment (ERA) in the late 1970s.

Scholar Susan Marshall (1985) documents the rhetoric and goals of anti-feminist movements in her aptly titled article "Ladies against women." The anti-suffrage movement was predominantly female with many of the women from the white, elite/upper class having husbands who were prominent politicians and industrialists (Marshall 1985; Schreiber 2017). While the first anti-suffrage movement formed in 1872, the years from 1912 to 1916 saw the most activism with around 350,000 members participating in the National Association Opposed to Woman Suffrage. While the members were opposed to many forms of progressive politics, a key issue for anti-feminists was to defend the status of homemaker. Marshall argues, "that the intersection of class and gender interests among many anti suffragists produced an ideology of woman as 'lady,' characterized by refinement, modesty, and domesticity ..." (1985: 350). These characterizations, along with the title of "lady," served to support traditional ideas of womanhood and femininity as removed from the public sphere of work and politics, and focused on the private sphere of home and family. In this way, anti-suffragists saw themselves as defending "true womanhood" and maintaining the support that women needed in society. Marshall describes their rhetoric in this way: "Woman suffrage symbolized the destruction of these distinct male and female spheres, forcing the sexes into competition and resulting in the loss of female power and privilege. Feminism was thus cast as an attack upon the right of females to lifetime financial support" (1985: 350). Indeed, the ability to vote was viewed by the anti-suffragists as a burden for women, and suffragists were seen as "not real women," or "freaks" who chose not to abide by their womanly nature. However committed in their opposition, one of the core dilemmas faced by anti-suffragists was how to preserve traditional femininity and womanhood within the private, home sphere that they claimed as their domain. For anti-suffragists this meant engaging in "quiet" politics of educating the public and avoiding parades, demonstrations, and speaking in public, all tactics embraced by suffragists (Marshall 1985). Scholars note that this form of "quiet" politics restrained anti-feminist efforts and led to their eventual defeat (Marshall 1985; Schreiber 2017). However, this was not the case in the countermovement to stop the ratification of the ERA.

The struggle to ratify the ERA came at a time of significant social change with the gay and lesbian, women's and civil rights movements all advocating for social change. Conservatives watched these changes with growing anxiety, and women were particularly concerned with some of the ways in which gender norms were changing (Schreiber 2017). While it seems counterintuitive that women would organize against a constitutional amendment making sex discrimination illegal, scholar Ronnee Schreiber argues that concern over social and cultural change and "savvy gender-identified organizing led to the defeat of the amendment" (2017: 320). Anti-ERA efforts began in earnest when it looked as though the amendment was going to be ratified, after passing through both houses of Congress and being successfully ratified in 22 states. Anti-ERA activists viewed feminists as degrading the homemaker and upsetting the natural separation of spheres where men ruled the public and women owned the private. Schreiber (2017) labels this gender ideology "maternalism," the view that women's main roles in society were as wives and mothers, valued for their domestic labor. The ERA was seen as an attempt to undo all of this, creating a gender-free society, spurred on by feminists who were characterized as "whiners" and who were disgruntled with their lives (Marshall 1985). The names of anti-ERA groups offer a clue as to members' belief in traditional gender norms. Groups such as Protect Our Womanhood (POW) and Happiness of Womanhood (HOW) arose. However, the most prominent group, STOP-ERA (Stop Taking Our Privileges-ERA), was organized by Phyllis Schafly. Schafly cast the ERA as legislation that would degrade women's protection and security as homemakers and add burdens to their lives. In addition, the ERA was portrayed by anti-ERA groups as giving men free rein to forsake their responsibilities to their families through easily accessible divorce.

Through the organizing efforts of STOP-ERA, activists wrote letters and sent their state legislators treats such as homemade bread, cookies, and jam, drawing on traditional womanhood (Marshall 1985). However, while anti-suffragists held quiet campaigns that relied on sympathetic men, the anti-ERA proponents did not hold back. Marshall writes, "Hence, unlike their predecessors, ERA opponents staged rallies, marches, and parades, although even here traditional legitimations were sometimes used, illustrated by the preponderance of antifeminist women with children at public gatherings. The image of ladylike dignity was also retained ..." (1985: 356). Much of the success of the anti-ERA forces is often credited to Schafly who had extensive political experience and traveled around the nation organizing groups (and continued to do so after the amendment's defeat in 1982). Feminists ironically noted that Schafly had gained much of that experience, as did other activists, due to the successful passage of women's suffrage in the 19th amendment.

Overall, these two countermovements – one failed and the other successful – drew on similar gender ideologies to resist the change that the women's movement advocated. Traditional womanhood was seen as confined to motherhood and family, dependent on men for support and valued for domestic labor. Marshall (1985) notes that "antifeminists of both eras expanded this theme to present themselves as defenders of the basic American values of

God and family, while portraying proponents of women's rights as sexually confused at best and subversive at worst" (359). While the anti-ERA and anti-suffrage participants are similar in some respects, they also departed in significant ways. While the anti-suffrage movement was made up of elite, educated women, the anti-ERA activists were more likely to be less educated, religious, married, older, and not employed. Race also played a role with women and men of color more likely to support the passage of the amendment, regardless of social class and education level.

Like societal backlash, movement–countermovement inter-actions can arise from the clashing of gender ideologies. While societal challenges around gender can spur backlash and counter-movements, so too can the very study of the gender concepts in academia.

Intellectual and popular backlash

As movements challenging gender norms have accomplished some of their goals, gender studies and women's studies programs have begun to face increasing attacks. Women's and gender studies programs began to appear in universities in the 1970s with the first academic journal started in 1972. These programs and the study of gender are the direct result of the rise of women's movements and the attacks against the movement and gender studies are directed at different, but related targets. One area of increasing attack is against what is called "identity politics" in academia and social movements. Identity politics are the result of groups of people coming to see each other as having a common social status or identity category. Movements by women, LGBTQ+ or other mar-ginalized communities are often labeled as "identity" movements versus larger, societal-wide movements that address issues cover-ing a range of people. In this light, identity movements/politics are seen as narrow in focus and ineffectual. Scholars respond to this criticism by noting how societal inequality creates marginalized groups who share an identity. This is particularly true around gender identities. "The wholesale rejection of identity politics by some as detracting from the real, structural, economic, and political roots of domination rests on an outdated view of gender as an individual attribute and an unwillingness to acknowledge the institutional basis of gender" (Reger, Taylor, and Whittier 1995: 16). In other words, when we understand gender as more than a personal trait, identity politics take on a much broader view of inequalities in society and cover a range of movements and goals.

Academia is also the site of criticism lodged against women and gender studies programs and departments (WGS) (sometimes called women's, gender and sexuality studies). Scholar Nancy Naples (2020) argues that these programs are under attack with their legitimacy as academic disciplines questioned. She argues that this is due, in part, to the programs' value being measured against the sciences, particularly around the ability to get grants and funding. Naples sees some of these attacks succeeding in eradicating gender programs through "austerity" measures that decrease funding, freeze budgets, and close down controversial programs in times of economic hardship. Other universities are less subtle and have outlawed, or tried to remove, gender studies programs. In 2018, Hungary, supported by right-wing sentiment, closed gender studies programs in the state-supported universities. A university official supported the closure saying, "The Hungarian government is of the clear view that people are born either men or women. They lead their lives the way they think best, but beyond this, the Hungarian state does not wish to spend public funds on education in this area" (Redden 2018: online). Naples (2020) views this closure as part of waves of resistance against gender theory sweeping across Europe and other parts of the world. In Poland, the minister of science and higher education is on record as opposing the official status of some gender and lesbian and gay-focused academic journals, noting that he viewed them as "pseudoscience" (Matthews 2017).

In 2017, noted theorist Judith Butler, who coined the concept of gender performativity, was burned in effigy outside a conference that she helped organize in Brazil (Jaschik 2017). The protest, organized by far-right Christian groups, called the gender theorist a "witch" and claimed that she was trying to undermine society by destroying people's gender identities. Protestors "held signs with her photo and phrases like 'Go to hell' (and far worse). Others held crosses and Brazilian flags in the air" (Jaschik 2017: online). Butler responded to the protest, saying:

> My sense is that the group who engaged in this frenzy of effigy burning, stalking, and harassment want to defend "Brazil" as a place where LGBTQ people are not welcome, where the family remains heterosexual (so no gay marriage), where abortion is illegal and reproductive freedom does not exist. They want boys to be boys, and girls to be girls, and for there to be no complexity in questions such as these. (Jaschik 2017: online)

Butler's response that the protestors want "boys to be boys and girls to be girls" reminds us how gender is a system of power in which gender categories are differentiated, ranked, and rewarded in a stratification system that underlies the social structure (Lorber 1994). These attacks on the programs and people who disseminate new ideas and understandings of gender serve as evidence of the power of that system. As of 2018, there was a bill pending in the Brazilian congress to bar the word "gender" in teaching.

Conclusion

This chapter examines how the advancement of gender, whether it concerns identities, policies, norms, or research, results in marginalization, backlash, and countermovements, and offers several key points. First, we can see how gender may be a binary used to organize the social world, but it is not how people live their lives. This tension between abiding by the binary and breaking it is evident in social movements such as the LGBTQ+ and women's movements. Returning to the discussion of same-sex marriage at the opening of the chapter, we can see how one of the divisions in the LGBTQ+ movement is around how to conceptualize gender as it relates to societal acceptance through issues around marriage and family versus the radical re-envisioning of society as seen in the potential of trans.

Yet, we have seen that as ideas around gender shift, so too do understandings of identity, sexuality, and gender expression. For example, the tactic of holding mass same-sex weddings at protests – discussed at the opening of the chapter – is an example of a social change effort used to bring about marriage, as well as other rights for lesbian and gay people. Verta Taylor and her co-authors (2009) argue that this tactic not only achieved cultural and political change but also forged a sense of solidarity and identity among participants that was central to the LGBTQ+ movement. In sum, standing in a crowd of same-sex couples, pledging to your relationship in public at a time when you were forbidden to marry, not only is a form of protest but it also changes the individuals who participate and commits them to the movement. When connections between individuals are made, communities form, and the culture and activism of these communities can bring change.

Second, we can see how as the gender binary begins to shift and the boundaries move, society changes in ways that benefit some and cause concern for others. While moving beyond the binary is a form of freedom for trans and gender non-conforming individuals, it does pose some dilemmas for movements organized around gender categories such as women's or men's movements. It is important to acknowledge the intense marginalization faced by trans men and women and gender non-conforming individuals within the women's and LGBTQ+ movements, as well as the larger society. Even when movements are welcoming, trans issues can be lost amid activist agendas. However, even inclusive feminists raise some concerns that they cannot lose focus on the gendered lives of women (cis and trans) and the barriers and discrimination that women as a group still face (Reger 2012). This results in some activists and academics asking: If gender is a key aspect of social structure, what does it mean to organize around the dissolving of the gender binary? Indeed, R. Clare Snyder (2008) argues that one of the key issues facing the women's movement is to address how trans women and men have complicated the category of "woman" and what that means to the goals of the movement. This complication concerns some feminists who are afraid of losing the category of "woman" in a world where women as a group still do not experience equality (Reger 2012; Stein 2010). Can feminist or women's movements exist without the idea of "woman" as a stable and defined category? The women's movement will continue to grapple with these questions.

These changes can bring backlash and countermovements develop to stop it. The history of social movements in any society is often the history of countermovements. The U.S. women's movement overall and the struggles for suffrage and the ERA are examples of how women and men mobilized to retain traditional ideas of femininity and womanhood. Even within movements that seek to change understandings of gender and sexuality, conflicts arise when one group advocates change the other does not want. This dynamic is evident in the rise of the trans social justice movement. Trans activists, in multiple movements, have struggled to open up definitions of gender, often in hostile spaces. As we have seen in other movements, when a movement shuts out one group, the result is often the emergence of another social justice movement.

Third, shifting ideas of gender that arise from movements can bring attacks on the very places these ideas are conceptualized and refined. The fact that gender theorists such as Judith Butler are seen as contributing to the decline of society and burned in effigy, and gender studies programs are under attack, is evidence of the power of gender in organizing our lives, our opportunities, and our access to power. Shifting the binary also shifts the gendered power structure of society, bringing equality or equity to some and reducing the privilege of others. As the gender binary shifts, it also brings with it the repositioning of other social identities such as race-ethnicity, social class, age, and others that are intertwined.

Sources to Explore

Faludi, Susan. 1991. *Backlash: The undeclared war against American women.* New York: Crown Publishers.

Feinberg, Leslie. 1993. *Stone butch blues.* Ithaca, NY: Firebrand Books.

Feinberg, Leslie. 1996. *Transgender warriors: Making history from Joan of Arc to RuPaul.* Boston: Beacon Press.

Schilt, Kristin and Laurel Westbrook. 2015. Bathroom battlegrounds and penis panics. *Contexts*, August. https://contexts.org/articles/bathroom-battlegrounds-and-penis-panics/

Westbrook, Laurel. 2020. *Unlivable lives: Violence and identity in transgender activism.* Berkeley, CA: University of California Press.

Anti-suffrage in the United States. https://www.nps.gov/articles/anti-suffragism-in-the-united-states.htm

Analysis of argument against the ERA. https://www.alicepaul.org/wp-content/uploads/2019/05/ERA-Anti-ERA-Arguments-08-2018.pdf

Questions to Consider

1. What is it about changing gender norms that can bring such heated backlash and countermovements? Can you think of examples of backlash happening in society today?

2. Select a gender norm that has changed over time. How was that gender norm a part of the social structure? Who was advantaged by the norm changing and who was disadvantaged?

3. How does the growing visibility of people living "beyond the binary" challenge gender norms in society? How does it open up gender for all people? Who is the most challenged by it?

4. What is the concern some feminists have with moving away from "woman" as a category to organize around? How is that concern embedded in countermovements?

5. Thinking about the world around you – what do you see in reactions to some of the gender lessons offered by academia?

Reflection

What are some societal changes you would like to see end or reverse? Is there a countermovement for that? Or a movement?

Conclusion:
Where Do We Go from Here?

Grandmothers of Plaza de Mayo.
Credit: Beatrice Murch/Flickr

Argentine President Cristina Fernandez Kirchner revealed the new $100 peso, which honored the Grandmothers of Plaza de Mayo. The Grandmothers are an activist organization that mobilized to find their disappeared children (activists put the number at 30,000) and their 500 grandchildren stolen at birth and illegally given away for adoption by

Argentina's last military regime (1976–1983). The military arrested people at home or off the street, including pregnant women or those with small children, then threw them into unmarked Ford Falcons; the majority were never seen again – hence, disappeared. President Fernandez, at the unveiling, said, "This is a tribute, which comes from the nation." One side of the bill shows a profile image of a Grandmother with the emblematic white scarf. The other side features the double helix of a DNA molecule in the middle, with a protest and a peace dove on one side and the silhouette of a headscarf on the other.

Quoted from Nicole Iturriaga (2019: 475)

Organized in 1977, the *Abuelas of de Plaza de Mayo* took to the streets to demand restitution for their kidnapped grandchildren and to know the location of their disappeared sons and daughters. In an attempt to repress subversives, Juan Perón's government kidnapped their children and had them adopted by military families. Clad in white headscarves, the grandmothers marched through the Plaza de Mayo in the Argentinian capital, Buenos Aires, demanding that their grandchildren, who were adopted by members of the military and political elite, be returned. In a public statement, they argued:

> The disappeared children were deprived of their identity, their religion, and their right to live with their family, in [other] words, all of the rights that are nationally and internationally recognized as their universal human rights. Our demand is concrete: that the children who were kidnapped as a method of political repression be restored to their legitimate families. (*Abuelas of the Plaza de Mayo*: online)

The collective action and eventual political recognition of the grandmothers is a story of collective resistance fueled by conventional ideas of gender. Using their gendered status as grandmothers and framing their strategies as one of family relations, these activists were able to launch a long-lived protest against a harsh and repressive regime. In some ways, this is the story of a victory with the activists nationally recognized and memorialized. In other ways, this is the story of defeat as the activists continue to search for their children and grandchildren, decades after their disappearance.[5] Their story of recognition and disappointment illustrates some of the core points of this volume. Drawing on their status as grandmothers, the activists illustrate how gendered people can organize in (largely) same-sex movements and draw on gendered networks, identities and ideas to organize protest. Their headscarves serve as gendered symbols of their activist identities and define who belongs to the group. To combat the gendered tactics of the regime, the elimination of subversives through the destruction of the family, they responded with a strategy that infused non-violent protest with norms of chivalry toward the elderly and women. They were able to continue their protests because of gendered stereotypes about activism and masculinity (i.e. "men are the 'real' activists") versus stereotypes about femininity/ womanhood and leadership (i.e. "women aren't leaders"). Yet those stereotypes kept their movement alive and the situation of their children and grandchildren public. As discussed in Chapter 2, the grandmothers were able to connect to each other emotionally and create networks to keep their movement alive. Overall, the Grandmothers of the Plaza de Mayo and their activism serves as a powerful reminder of the intertwining of gender and social movements as discussed through this book. Yet we have seen how drawing on conventional gender norms and expectations in the form of grandmothers and mothers can stymie a movement, when women return home and take up conventional roles.

Gender transgressions, pushing against gender norms, often offer the promise of more radical change. The gender rebel drag queens in the twentieth-century U.S. LGBTQ+ movement fought for equality around sexuality, at the same time they pushed against the gender binary. Yet, as we saw in the case of Sylvia Rivera in Chapter 5, those rebels can face harsh criticism and treatment from others in the movement. It should also be clear that the activists of one generation leave a legacy for the next even if they face hostility in their own time. These two cases – the *abuelas* of Argentina and the gender pioneers of the U.S. LGBTQ+ movement – highlight some of the core questions about gender and social movements raised in the book. I address those questions below.

Is Gender Still Relevant in Social Movements?

In a list of the largest coordinated marches in U.S. history, the women's marches of 2017 (with at least 4.2 million participating) and 2018 (with at least 2.2 million) were protests that overtly focused on aspects of gender discrimination, as well as other issues (Kauffman 2018). With their myriad of gender-related issues such as sexism, employment discrimination, sexual harassment, rape, and sexual violence, the women's marches illustrate how multiple aspects of gender inequality continue to be articulated through social protest. Many of the issues raised in the 2017 and 2018 marches were articulated because of past movements. I began this book with a scenario based on the #MeToo movement and its roots in U.S. feminism to illustrate how gender issues can remain a source of protest over generations of activists, both changing the world and contributing to future change. Chapter 1 demonstrates how, as the social world changes, those changes can inspire social protest. Indeed, scholars remind us that despite the wide range of goals embraced by women's movements around the world, they flourish in periods of generalized social upheaval (Chafe 1977; Taylor and Whittier 1997) with changes in the social structure sparking women's activism (Chafetz and Dworkin 1986; Huber and Spitze 1983; Klein 1984). Factors such as increases in labor force participation and educational attainment, the ability to control reproduction and fertility, and/or changes in the shape and structure of the family can all bring collective action working to bring about or stop change (Chafetz and Dworkin 1986; Ferree and Hess 1985/1995; Klein 1984). As Amrita Basu (2017) notes, when women's lives change, they are able to organize collectively against injustice and oppression in their lives and communities. The popular media also confirms this idea with the work of reporters Nicholas Kristof and Sheryl WuDunn, who argue that women who gain control over their lives are able to work collectively to challenge societal conditions such as slavery, female circumcision, and illiteracy (2010). In sum, as the world changes, it brings with it the need to realign our understanding of gender, drawing on generations of activists in the process.

We can also see how gender remains important in movements that embrace a variety of goals and how, when some of those goals are accomplished, society changes. The U.S. women's movement provides an example where goals have shifted, and generations have been involved. In the twenty-first century, women and men come to feminism in a society dramatically shaped by the feminist generations that came before them. As children they may have read gender-neutral children's books, attended summer camps organized around gender equity, and entered universities and colleges offering women's and/or gender studies classes. As a result, contemporary feminists in the United States continue to work in the formal organizations started by the previous generation, such as domestic violence shelters, rape crisis centers, women's centers on campuses, but also embraced new forms of feminist activism often embedded in their everyday routines and activities (Reger 2012).

Men's movements, though not as long-lived as women's movements, have also created generations of activists that continue to work on shifting issues. Michael Messner and his co-authors (2015) identify multiple generations of men engaged in antiviolence work. They identify a "movement" cohort from the 1970s and 1980s, a "bridge" cohort from the 1980s to 1990s and a "professional" cohort from the mid 1990s that continues today. These cohorts of activists brought antiviolence work from grass-root organizing to institutionalized programs, setting up a path to make a career out of addressing issues of violence. Just as women's movements are often the result of changes in society, so too are men's movements. Messner and colleagues note that the women's movement brought a shift in society that "occurred with the force and speed of a powerful earthquake, jarring the foundations of how people thought about violence against women" and spurring on antiviolence activism by men (2015: 13).

While gender is apparent in single-gender movements, as covered in Chapter 2, social movements often embrace non-gendered goals. For example, returning to the list of U.S. marches (Kaufmann 2018:

91), other large coordinated protests include the Moratorium to End the War in Vietnam in 1969, the Nationwide Student Strike against the War in 1970, The "World Says No to War" protests in 2003, Immigrant Rights Protests in 2006, Student Walkouts on Gun Violence in 2018 and the March for Our Lives (against gun violence) in 2018. The 2020 #BlackLivesMatter protests, spread across the United States, are estimated to be some of the largest protests ever in the history of the country, with an estimated 15–26 million people participating around the world (Buchanan, Bui and Patel 2020). These are all multi-gender movements that drew extraordinarily large numbers of participants. Yet, despite the focused attention on gender, we have seen how gender remains relevant in movements in the potential for participants, to the dynamics within the movement to the pathways followed.

How Does Gender Organize Social Movements?

By focusing on the movement and groups that organized these protests, we can see how gender in a movement moves beyond a connection to the sex category of the participants and their gendered lives. Instead, by examining the differences between how men and women fare in movements, we can see how gender constrains some and provides opportunities to others. Those constraints and opportunities can result from the expectations of others *and* internalized ideas of appropriate behavior through gender socialization. Indeed, when we can see how women and men fare differently in movements, we can see how gender structures and organizes all of society. These societal expectations and behaviors – the process of "doing gender" – are organized in a stratification system and embedded in social structures that shape our lives.

Overall, multi-gender movements tell us what it means to live and interact in a gendered world and that the gender stratification that exists outside of movements also exists within it. Women, and other marginalized identities, have experienced discrimination within movements, from having their issues not being taken seriously to not being seen as "real" activists. When women are viewed as activists, it is often through the lens of traditional gender roles. As such, women are often studied in movements through their roles as mothers. Men, on the other hand, are often portrayed as "warriors" in the movement, with their masculinity and the influence of gender unexplored. In contrast to women and motherhood, masculinity and the way it shapes activism remains largely invisible in the research. In addition, taking an intersectional perspective reveals how straight, white men are often the focus of research, with their gender unexplored. Overall, gender organizes movements from the individual to the societal and is embedded in their structures and cultures.

How are Key Aspects of Social Movements Influenced?

Whereas Chapter 2 focuses on multi-gender movements to illustrate how gender stratification operates in movements, Chapter 3 moves the focus to some of the key concerns of social movement scholars – recruitment and mobilization – illustrating how gender stratification can affect who participates in a movement. One key process of the gender stratification system is the creation of difference. When differences between men and women are ranked and then rewarded differently, a stratification system is put into place. Gender stratification in movements means that activist identities that incorporate gender also incorporate inequality. In other words, the ways in which people come into movements is shaped by gender constraints and opportunities also experienced in their social world. Men and women continue to live different lives within the realms of work and family (Hochschild 1989), and those differences contribute to differences in their personal or biographical availability. Women often experience either real or perceived barriers to joining a social movement due to their roles in society. Along with personal, family, and work obligations, the networks to which men and women belong differ, resulting in different paths to activism. The messages or frames that social movement leaders send to potential recruits are also gendered, with women's identities as nurturers or protectors of the family being called upon, whereas men's frames focus on risk and masculinity. While these frames might be appealing to women who are mothers, or men in terms of their perceived manliness, frames that are tightly gendered to a specific role or idea leave out those who do not see themselves, or resonate with the ideas presented, particularly those outside the binary. These dynamics – availability, networks, and frames – result in differing paths to mobilization for men and women.

While gendered constraints and opportunities for women and men can shape how they come to movements, Chapter 4 explores how gender shapes their experiences within movements. As Arlie Hochschild notes, we experience the world around us "given the cultural notions of gender at play" (1989: 15). Life within the movement often reflects the gender norms outside the movement. Leadership is a key area where, to borrow Hochschild's observation, "gender is at play." Women either experience barriers to assuming positions of leadership or do a style of leadership that is not acknowledged by others in the movement (and sometimes by scholars who study them). These barriers are based on gendered assumptions of who a leader is (often a man) and how leaders conduct themselves (often as hierarchical and dominant). Studies of the civil rights movements illustrate how these assumptions missed the important organizing and leadership roles that women carried out in their communities. Drawing only on mainstream ideas of leadership when considering gender, race, and class leaves out those who are not middle or upper class, white, male, and masculine. While it is tempting to argue that the days when those leadership barriers existed are gone, work on the relatively recent Occupy movement indicates that barriers to leadership continue to exist for women and those outside the gender binary.

Leaders live in a gendered world and consequently can draw on gendered assumptions in the creation of strategies and tactics. One example of this is the Freedom Summer campaign where men and women were given different (gendered) jobs as part of the overall strategy of the SNCC. While the strategy was non-violent civil disobedience and community work, the tactics were gendered, with men and women predominantly working separately for voting rights. In sum, gender is evident in the strategies and tactics of a movement, not only in the gender of the person doing or designing the action but also in the connotations of the action and tactic. Overall, social movements, no matter what their goal, are gendered universes that shape who assumes positions in the movement and the strategies and tactics activists use to make change.

How Do People Respond to the Binary?

While movements replicate societal norms of gender, they also have the ability to challenge, and potentially change, gender norms. It is clear that gender is a cultural and political system of stratification and structures, yet people in (and out) of social movements often do not align with societal ideas of gender. Indeed, that is a core tension in the previous chapters – how do we understand the gender binary as a tool for organizing society while the gender identities of activists do not always align to the binary? While the disruption of the gender binary is incorporated into the everyday life of individuals, it is also a key aspect of social movements. The women's movement challenged traditional gender norms and helped to expand aspects of the gender binary. Protests and dissension in the LGBTQ+ movement helped set the stage for the revision of the traditional family, breaking down some of the gender stereotypes, while continuing to support heteronormative ideals. We now live in a time where the gender binary feels more flexible than ever before and transgender and gender nonconforming people work in a myriad of social justice groups and organizations. While the relationship between transgender and gender non-conforming activists and the women's and LGBTQ+ movement has been tumultuous and problematic, work within these movements has helped change norms on gender expression and identity and human rights. Yet, as addressed in Chapter 5, as movements work to change gender norms and ideologies, they also can experience resistance from both inside and out-side. For example, some feminists, clinging to essentialist ideas of sex, reject transgender women and men from women's movement organizations and communities (Stryker 2017). LGBTQ+ move-ments can abandon the "T" when transgender rights do not align with the goals of organizational donors. Outside the movement, backlash can come in a variety of forms. Mainstream society, through culture and institutions, can actively work to undo the gains of movements, as is evident in the backlash against feminism (Faludi 1991). Movements can organize with the goal of oppos-ing the gains and desired outcomes of another. As was evident in the countermovements opposing suffrage and later the ERA, the battle is often about defining gendered norms and an "appropri-ately" gendered life. For women working against suffrage, being a woman meant that the burden of public and political life should be avoided. For the women working against the ERA, public and political life was allowed (to some degree) but the protections guaranteed women by the norms of femininity needed defending. Both anti-suffrage and anti-ERA activists sought to stop feminist redefinition of what it meant to be a woman in society.

The backlash in society against changes in gender has spilled over into the study of gender itself. Recognizing the revolutionary potential of questioning how we experience the world through gender and seeing beyond the binary leads to some places in the world where gender studies are seen as destroying a key part of the foundation of society. When we consider how feminism brought gender studies to the academy, we can see how, once again, gender and social movements are linked. Challenging gender opens up the world, but it also threatens the social order in a profound way.

What Does the Study of Gender Bring to Social Movements (and Vice Versa)?

Throughout this book, I have focused on three main themes. The primary goal is to show how gender and social movements are intertwined and influence each other, and to do that I have drawn on a wide range of research. At the same time, another theme has been how the study of gender and social movement research inform each other and what the gaps in the research are. This is not to say that scholars have not integrated gender into social movement theories. A score of research illustrates how adding gender to social movement concepts and theories adds new insights. For example, adding gender to the analysis expands ideas of leadership, goals, strategies, tactics, outcomes, and movement continuity. The U.S. women's movement has been a particularly fruitful place for these theoretical insights. For example, by studying the U.S. women's movement, researchers examine how gender is a form of power. Taylor and Staggenborg argue that gender inequality is "one of the most fundamental relations of power" and that bringing gender into research demonstrates how power is contested (2005: 48). Indeed, Staggenborg and Taylor use the U.S. women's movement to re-conceptualize the very nature of social movements.

While gender has expanded conceptions of social movements, social movement research has contributed to gender scholarship. Social movements such as the transgender social justice movement add important dimensions to how gender is conceptualized by defining and refining the ways in which gender is expressed and labeled. For example, the use of the pronoun "they" as singular, referring to a range of gender identities, is an outcome of this movement, which expands the gender binary and allows for a range of gender expressions. As noted earlier, examining social movements through a gender lens also illustrates how femininity and womanhood are often identified but masculinity and manhood are often left unexamined or invisible. The use of the non-gendered activist in studies perpetuates the stereotype of men as the "default" or unidentified actors. In sum, to return to Staggenborg and Taylor (2005), what gender and social movements have in common is an examination and articulation of power in society. Differing gender norms indicate power differentials and social movements attempt to redistribute power. When they are considered in conjunction with each other, they offer valuable insights to scholarship but, more importantly, they illustrate one of the key ways the social world is organized.

A third theme in this book has been the importance of adopting intersectionality as a lens through which to view social movements. As many studies have illustrated, the temptation to focus only on gender ignores the complexity of social life. The "Wall of Moms" in the 2020 Black Lives Matter protest illustrates how important it is to look beyond gender. By strategically positioning moms, most of them white, in front of other protestors, organizers drew on multiple social understandings and stereotypes. Without an intersectional perspective, race and racism disappear from this tactic, leaving only a one-dimensional comprehension of the movement's goals. By situating people fully in their social context and acknowledging how race-ethnicity, class, age, sexual orientation among other identities shape lives, we can also see how social movements are shaped. Rachel Einwohner and colleagues (2000) encourage us to see the variability in gender through an intersectional lens. They write:

> We suggest that gender is not a static or objective protest tool; instead, its meaning is heavily dependent on the broader social and political context. Gender is constructed and enacted by actors within cultures and is therefore dynamic and flexible. The substance of gender can vary across cultures. In addition, it may vary across the same culture at different points in time and across different groups within the same culture. (2000: 694)

Included in an intersectional lens is the need to take a global perspective. The opening scenario of this chapter of the Grandmothers of the Plaza de Mayo reminds us of the commonalities and differences in social movements organizing around the world. The grandmothers draw on gender to protest but do so in a unique social setting, shaped by national and global dynamics. Scholar Cynthia Enloe argues that "[t]o make sense of today's complex world, we need to understand that many decisions have not only gendered *consequences* but gendered *causes* – that is, causes flowing from presumptions or fears about femininity or masculinity" (2007: 17 [emphasis in the original]). While Enloe argues that gender can be a starting point for understanding the complexity of the global world, M. Bahati Kuumba notes that a global analysis can be the start of a fruitful analysis around gender. She notes:

> One of the most exciting trends in the development of gendered social movement research is the placement of gender struggles and women's activism within the context of globalized systems ... Neither social policy nor social activism is currently confined to the nation-state level. (2001: 139)

By considering how gender and social movement research inform each other, as well as the importance of looking through an intersectional and global lens, it is evident that gender and social movements intertwine in meaningful ways, informing the social world we live in. Gender combines with other social identities shaping how people fare in society and movements. A global perspective of movements needs to bring with it a gendered analysis. Movements change notions of gender, and gender shapes the work of movements. To understand the two together is to acknowledge how power is distributed in society and the work that activists do to redistribute that power. That work happens in our interactions with each other, the networks and kinship systems we live in, the organizations we join and the strategies and tactics we enact to make change. Gendered and gender generic social movements have changed the contours of the world we live in and will continue to shape us and our social worlds.

To conclude, thinking about gender in social movements (and vice versa) allows us to realize some of the ways in which gender constrains us and the practices by which this happens. Gender and work scholar Patricia Yancey Martin argues that "attention to practices of gender will produce insights into how inequalities are created" (2003: 343). Martin's work focuses on how bureaucratic workplaces maintain gender inequality; however, her work offers guidelines to eradicating the harmful effects of that inequality. She argues that gender can be seen as a system of action that sustains relationships and consequently, reinforces institutions. She labels this process, "the saying and doing [that] create what is said and done" (2003: 352). To interrupt gender inequality, Martin argues for attention to the practicing of gender; in other words, how it is done and redone through our often-unconscious interactions. She encourages us to examine a multitude of practices – from agency/intentionality/awareness/reflexivity – to positions/power/experience to choice/accountability/experience. In sum, Martin calls us to address the invisible and visible ways in which gender is embedded in our lives. I would add that focusing on the ways in which we change that social life through social movements is a good place to start.

Notes

1 The Chinese Exclusion Act of 1862 was in place until 1943 and was the first major law restricting immigration in the United States. https://www.history.com/topics/immigration/chinese-exclusion-act-1882
2 At this time, the majority of counties in Mississippi had Black populations ranging from 16 to over 50 percent.
3 It is important to note that issues of gender and race led to multiple debates about the use of the walls of moms and dads and many of these debates played out on Twitter.
4 Penis panics arise from the societal belief that male bodies belong to inherent predators and no man is free from this assumption. Trans women are also included in this. Cisgender women then are vulnerable and weak, always potential victims, particularly in public restrooms. See Schilt and Westbrook 2015.
5 Over the course of three decades approximately 120 children were located. It is estimated that up to 500 children were kidnapped. The organization continues to push for methods to locate and identify the missing children.

References

Abelson, Miriam, 2019. Already feminists: Trans feminist histories, hurdles, and futures, pp. 43–59 in Jo Reger (ed.) *Nevertheless, they persisted: Feminisms and continued resistance in the U.S. women's movement.* New York: Routledge.

Abuelas de Plaza de Mayo. History of the *Abuelas de Plaza de Mayo.* https://abuelas.org.ar/idiomas/english/history.htm

Acker, Joan. 1990. Hierarchy, jobs, bodies: A theory of gendered organizations. *Gender & Society* 4:2: 139–158.

Adams, Jacqueline. 2002. Gender and social movement decline: Shantytown women and the prodemocracy movement in Pinochet's Chile. *Journal of Contemporary Ethnography* 31:3: 285–322.

Aminzade, Ron and Doug McAdam, D. 2001. Emotions and contentious politics, pp. 14–50 in Ron R. Aminzade, Jack A. Goldstone, Doug McAdam, Elizabeth J. Perry, William H. Sewell Jr., Sidney Tarrow, and Charles Tilly (eds.) *Silence and the voice in the study of contentious politics.* Cambridge, MA: Cambridge University Press.

Bagguley, Paul. 2002. Contemporary British feminism: A social movement in abeyance? *Social Movement Studies* 1:2: 169–185.

Baker, Carrie N. 2018. *Fighting the US youth sex trade: Gender, race and politics.* Cambridge, UK: Cambridge University Press.

Banaszak, Lee Ann and Holly McCammon. 2018. Epilogue: Women's activism from electoral campaigns to protest action: Into the next 100 years, pp. 356–369 in Holly McCammon and Lee Ann Banaszak (eds.) *100 years of the Nineteenth Amendment: An appraisal of women's political activism.* New York: Oxford University Press.

Barnett, Bernice McNair. 1993. Invisible southern black women leaders in the civil rights movement: The triple constraints of gender, race, and class. *Gender & Society* 7:2: 162–182.

Basu, Amrita. 2017. Introduction, pp. 1–33 in Amrita Basu (ed.) *Women's* movements in the global era: The power of local feminisms. New York: Westview Press.

Baumgardner, Jennifer and Amy Richards. 2000. Manifesta: Young women, feminism and the future. New York: Farrar, Straus, Giroux.

Beckwith, Karen. 1996. Lancashire women against pit closures: Women's standing in a men's movement. Signs: A Journal of Culture and Society 21:4: 1034–1068.

Bell, Shannon Elizabeth. 2013. Our roots run deep as Ironweed: Appalachian women and the fight for environmental justice. Urbana, IL: University of Illinois Press.

Bell, Shannon Elizabeth, and Yvonne A. Braun. 2010. Coal, identity, and the gendering of environmental justice activism in central Appalachia. Gender & Society 24: 6: 794–813.

Bellafante, Ginia. 1998. Is feminism dead? Time Magazine 151: 25. http://www.time.com/time/magazine/article/0,9171,988616-2,00.html

Beyerlein, Kraig and Bergstrand, Kelly. 2013. Biographical availability. Online in David A. Snow, Donna Della Porta, Bert Klandermans, and Doug McAdam (eds.) The Wiley-Blackwell encyclopedia of social and political movements. Wiley Online Library. https://onlinelibrary.wiley.com/action/showCitFormats?doi=10.1002%2F9780470674871.wbespm012

Beyerlein, Kraig, and John Hipp. 2006. A two-stage model for a two-stage process: How biographical availability matters for social movement mobilization. Mobilization: An International Quarterly 11:3: 299–320.

Black Lives Matter. 2020. About. https://blacklivesmatter.com/about/

Blee, Kathy. 2003. Inside organized racism: Women in the hate movement. Berkeley: University of California Press.

Blum, Dani. 2020. "The Moms are here": "Wall of Moms" groups mobilize nationwide. New York Times, July 27. https://www.nytimes.com/2020/07/27/parenting/wall-of-moms-protests.html

Bosco, Fernando J. 2006. The Madres de Plaza do Mayo and three decades of human rights activism: Embeddedness, emotions and social movements. Annals of the Association of American Geographers, 96:2: 342–365.

Bridges, Tristan. 2010. Men just weren't made to do this: Performances of drag at "Walk a Mile in Her Shoes" marches. Gender & Society 24:1: 5–30.

Bridges, Tristan. 2021. Antifeminism, profeminism, and the myth of white men's disadvantage. Signs: Journal of Culture and Society. 46: 3: 663–688.

Bridges, Tristan and C. J. Pascoe. 2014. Hybrid masculinities: New directions in the sociology of men and masculinities. Sociology Compass 8:3: 246–258.

Bridges, Tristan and C. J. Pascoe. 2018. On the elasticity of gender hegemony: Why hybrid masculinities fail to undermine gender and sexual inequality, pp. 254–274 in James W. Messerschmidt, Michael A. Messner, Raewyn Connell, and Patricia Yancey Martin (eds.) Gender reckonings: New social theory and research. New York: NYU Press.

References

Brooks, Kim. 2020. Feminism has failed women. *New York Times*, December 23. https://www.nytimes.com/2020/12/23/opinion/coronavirus-women-feminism.html

Buchanan, Larry, Quoctrung Bui, and Jugal K. Patel. 2020. Black Lives Matter may be the largest movement in U.S. history. *New York Times*, July 3. https://www.nytimes.com/interactive/2020/07/03/us/george-floyd-protests-crowd-size.html

Buechler, Steven M. 1990. *Women's movements in the United States*. New Brunswick, N.J.: Rutgers University Press.

Cable, Sherry. 1992. Women's social movement involvement: The role of structural availability in recruitment and participation processes. *The Sociological Quarterly* 33:1: 35–50.

Cappelli, Mary L. 2020. Black Lives Matter: The emotional and racial dynamics of the George Floyd protest graffiti. *Advances in Applied Sociology* 10: 323–347.

Castillo, Rosalva Aida Hernández. 2010. Toward a culturally situated women's rights agenda: Reflections from Mexico, pp. 315–342 in Amrita Basu (ed.) *Women's movements in the global era: The power of local feminisms* Boulder, CO: Westview Press.

Chafe, William H. 1977. *Women and equality: Changing patterns in American culture*. New York: Oxford University Press.

Chafetz, Janet S. and Dworkin Anthony G. 1986. *Female revolt: Women's movements in world and historical perspective*. Totowa, N.J.: Rowman and Allanheld.

Chan, Jody and Joe Curnow. 2017. Taking up space: Men, masculinity, and the student climate movement. *RCC Perspectives* 4: 77–86.

Chappell, Bill. 2015. Supreme Court declares same-sex marriage legal in all 50 states, *NPR*. https://www.npr.org/sections/thetwo-way/2015/06/26/417717613/supreme-court-rules-all-states-must-allow-same-sex-marriages

Chatelain, Marcia and Kayya Asoka. 2015. Women and Black Lives Matter. *Dissent* 63:3: 54–61.

Chatillon, Anna and Beth E. Schneider. 2018. "We must summon the courage": Black activist mothering against police brutality. Marginalized mothers, mothering from the margins. *Advances in Gender Research* 25: 245–258.

Coe, Anna-Britt and Linda Sandberg. 2019. Gender beliefs as a dimension of tactical choice: The 'Take Back the Night' march in Sweden. *Social Movement Studies* 18:5: 622–638.

CODEPINK. 2019. How did we get started? https://www.codepink.org/about

Collins, Patricia Hill. 1990. *Black feminist thought: Knowledge, consciousness, and the politics of empowerment*. Boston, MA Unwin Hyman.

Combahee River Collective. 1978. The Combahee River Collective statement, © by Zillah Eisenstein. http://circuitous.org/scraps/combahee.html

Connell, Raewyn. 2016. Masculinities in global perspective: Hegemony, contestation, and changing structures of power. *Theory and Society* 45: 303–318.

Connell, Raewyn. 1995. *Masculinities*. Berkeley and Los Angeles: University of California Press.

Connell, Raewyn. 1987. *Gender and power: Society, the person and sexual politics*. Stanford, CA: Stanford University Press.

Corte, Ugo, and Bob Edwards. 2008. White power and the mobilization of racist social movements. *Music and Arts in Action* 1: online. https://musicandartsinaction.net/index.php/maia/article/view/whitepowermusic/9

Costain, Anne. 1992. *Inviting women's rebellion: A political interpretation of the women's movement*. Baltimore, MD: John Hopkins University Press.

Crenshaw, Kimberlé. 1991. Mapping the margins: Identity politics, intersectionality, and violence against women. *Stanford Law Review* 43:6: 1241–1299.

Crenshaw, Kimberlé W. and Andrea J. Ritchie (with Rachel Anspach and Rachel Gilmer). 2015. *Say Her Name*, African American Policy Forum, Center for Intersectionality and Social Policy Studies, New York.

Crossley, Alison Dahl. 2019. Online feminism is just feminism: Offline and online movement persistence, pp. 60–78 in Jo Reger (ed.) *Nevertheless, they persisted: Feminisms and continued resistance in the U.S. women's movement*. New York: Routledge.

Crossley, Alison Dahl. 2017. *Finding feminism: Millennial activists and the unfinished gender revolution*. New York: NYU Press.

Curtis, Charlotte. 1968. Miss America pageant picketed by 100 women. *New York Times*, September 8, 1968, 81.

Davis, Heath Fogg. 2017. *Beyond trans: Does gender matter?* New York: NYU Press.

D'Emilo, John. 1998. *Sexual politics, sexual communities: The making of a homosexual minority in the United States, 1940–1970*. Chicago: University of Chicago Press.

De Onis, Juan. 1971. "The world." *New York Times* archives, December 5, 1971. https://www.nytimes.com/1971/12/05/archives/the-ominous-pounding-of-pots-chile.html

DuBois, Ellen C. 1978. *Feminism and suffrage: The emergence of an independent women's movement in America 1848–1869*. Ithaca, N.Y.: Cornell University Press.

Echols, Alice. 1989. *Daring to be bad: Radical feminism in America 1967–1975*. Minneapolis: University of Minnesota Press.

Edwards, Stassa. 2015. Mount Holyoke cancels "The Vagina Monologues" for transgender students, January 15. *Jezebel*. https://jezebel.com/mount-holyoke-cancels-the-vagina-monologues-for-trans-1679845927

Einwohner, Rachel. 1999. Gender, class and social movement outcomes: Identity and effectiveness in two animal rights campaigns. *Gender & Society* 13:1: 56–76.

References

Einwohner, Rachel L., Jocelyn A. Hollander, and Toska Olson. 2000. Engendering social movements: Cultural images and movement dynamics. *Gender & Society* 14:5: 679–699.

Enloe, Cynthia. 2007. *Globalization and militarism: Feminists make the link.* Lanham, MD: Rowman and Littlefield.

Essof, Sheeren. 2010. *Ramagwana Rakajeka*: Opportunities and challenges of the Zimbabwean women's movement, pp 57–88 in Amrita Basu (ed.) *Women's movements in the global era: The power of local feminisms.* Boulder, CO: Westview Press.

Evans, Sara M. 1980. *Personal politics: The roots of women's liberation in the civil rights movement and the new left.* New York: Vintage Books.

Faludi, Susan. 1991. *Backlash: The undeclared war against American women.* New York: Crown Publishers.

Farrell, Warren. 1993. *The myth of male power: Why men are the disposable sex.* New York: Simon and Schuster.

Farrell, Warren. 1974. *The liberated man.* New York: Random House.

Ferree, Myra M. 2004. Soft repression: Ridicule, stigma, and silencing in gender-based movements, pp. 85–101 in Daniel J. Myers and Daniel M. Cress (eds.) *Authority in Contention, Research in Social Movements, Conflict and Change.* Boston, MA: Elsevier.

Ferree, Myra M. and Beth B. Hess. 1985/1995. *Controversy and coalition: The new feminist movement across three decades of change.* New York: Twayne.

Ferree, Myra M. and Carol McClurg Mueller. 2004. Feminism and the women's movement: A global perspective, pp. 576–607 in David Snow, Sarah A. Soule, and Hanspeter Kriesi (eds.) *The Blackwell Companion to Social Movements.* Oxford, UK: Blackwell.

Ferree, Myra Marx and Silke Roth. 1998. Gender, class, and the interaction between social movements: A strike of West Berlin day care workers. *Gender & Society* 12:6: 626–648.

Finn, Natalie, 2020. "How Black Lives Matter began: Meet the women whose hashtag turned into a global movement." E News. https://www.eonline.com/news/1158910/how-black-lives-matter-began-meet-the-women-whose-hashtag-turned-into-a-global-movement

Flood, Michael. 2005. Men's collective struggles for gender justice. The case of antiviolence activism, pp. 458–465 in Michael Kimmel, Jeff Hearn, and Raewyn Connell, (eds.) *Handbook of studies on men and masculinities.* Thousand Oaks, CA: Sage Publications.

Fonow, Mary Margaret. 1998. Protest engendered: The participation of women steelworkers in the Wheeling-Pittsburgh Steel Strike of 1985. *Gender & Society* 12:6: 710–728.

Freeman, Jo. 1975. *The politics of women's liberation: A case study of an emerging social movement and its relation to the policy process.* New York: Longman.

References

Freeman, Jo. 1973. The origins of the women's liberation movement. *American Journal of Sociology* 78.4: 792–811.

Friedan, Betty. 1963. *The feminine mystique*. New York: W.W. Norton and Co.

Gaby, Sarah and Neal Caren. 2015. Online Occupy: How cute old men and Malcolm X recruited 400,000 U.S. users to OWS on Facebook, pp. 88–95 in Jenny Pickerill, John Krinsky, Graeme Hayes, Kevin Gillan, and Brian Doherty (eds.) *Occupy! A Global Movement*. London: Routledge.

Galli, Anya. 2016. How glitter bombing lost its sparkle: The emergence and decline of a novel social movement tactic. *Mobilization: An International Quarterly* 21:3: 259–282.

Gamson, William. 1992. *Talking politics*. New York: Cambridge University Press.

Ganz, Marshall. 2000. Resource and resourcefulness: Strategic capacity in the unionization of California agriculture, 1956–1966. *American Journal of Sociology* 105:4: 1003–1062.

Garrison, Ednie Kaeh. 2005. Are we on a wavelength yet? On feminist oceanography, radios and third wave feminism, pp. 237–256 in Jo Reger (ed.) *Different wavelengths: Studies of the contemporary women's movement*. New York: Routledge.

Gerber, Lynne. 2015. Grit, guts, and vanilla beans: Godly masculinity in the ex-gay movement. *Gender & Society* 29:1: 26–50.

Gerson, Judith M. and Kathy Peiss. 1985. Boundaries, negotiation, consciousness: Reconceptualizing gender relations. *Social Problems* 32:4: 317–331.

Giele, Janet Zollinger. 1995. *Two paths to women's equality: Temperance, suffrage and the origins of modern feminism*. New York: Twayne Publishers.

Goldberg, Herb. 1976. *The hazards of being male: Surviving the myth of masculine privilege*. New York: Signet.

Goodwin, Jeff, James Jasper, and Francesca Polletta (eds.). 2001. *Political passions: Emotions and social movements*. Chicago: University of Chicago Press.

Hairgrove, Frank and Douglas M. Mcleod. 2008. Circles drawing toward high risk activism: The use of *Usroh* and *Halaqa* in Islamist radical movements. *Studies in Conflict & Terrorism*, 31:5: 399–411.

Hawkesworth, Mary. 2004. The semiotics of premature burial: Feminism in a postfeminist age. *Signs: Journal of Culture and Society* 29: 961–986.

Hayden, Casey and Mary King. 1965. Sex and caste: A kind of memo, p. 227 in Judith Papachristou (ed.) *Women together: A history in documents of the women's movement in the United States*. New York: Alfred Knopf.

Heath, Melanie. 2003. Soft-boiled masculinity: Renegotiating gender and racial ideologies in the Promise Keepers movement. *Gender & Society* 17:3: 423–444.

Hercus, Cheryl. 1999. Identity, emotion and feminist collective action. *Gender & Society* 13:1: 34–55.

Hermann, Peter, Marissa Lang, and Clarence Williams. 2020. Pro-Trump rally descends into chaos as Proud Boys roam D.C. looking to fight. *Washington*

Post, December 13. https://www.washingtonpost.com/local/public-safety/proud-boys-protest-stabbing-arrest/2020/12/13/98c0f740-3d3f-11eb-8db8-395dedaaa036_story.html

Hines, Sally. 2005. "I am a feminist but…": Transgender men, women and feminism, pp. 57–78 in Jo Reger (ed.) *Different wavelengths: Studies of the contemporary women's movement*. New York: Routledge.

Hochschild, Arlie. 1989. *The second shift: Working parents and the revolution at home*. New York: Random House.

Hochschild, Arlie. 1983. *The managed heart: Commercialization of human feeling*. Berkeley: University of California Press.

hooks, bell. 1989. *Talking back: Thinking feminist, thinking black*. Boston: South End Press.

Honey, Michael K. 2007. *Going down Jericho Road: The Memphis strike, Martin Luther King's last campaign*. New York: W.W. Norton.

Huber, Joan and G. Spitze. 1983. *Sex stratification: Children, housework and jobs*. New York: Academic Press.

Hunt, Scott A., Robert D. Benford, and David A. Snow. 1994. Identity fields: Framing processes and the social construction of movement identities, pp. 185–208 in Enrique Larana, Hank Johnston, and Joseph R. Gusfield (eds.) *New social movements: From ideology to identity*. Philadelphia: Temple University Press.

Hunt, Swanee and Cristina Posa. 2001. Women waging peace. *Foreign Policy* 124: (May–June): 38–47.

Hurwitz, Heather McKee. 2019. Gender and race in the Occupy Movement: Relational leadership and discriminatory resistance. *Mobilization: An International Quarterly* 24: 2: 157–176.

Hussey, Rebecca. 2018 Ten new books on anger, feminism and unruly women. *Book Riot*, September 26. https://bookriot.com/new-books-on-anger-feminism-and-unruly-women/

Iturriaga, Nicole. 2019. The evolution of the Grandmothers of Plaza De Mayo's mnemonic framing. *Mobilization: An International Quarterly* 24:4: 475–492

Irons, Jenny. 1998. The shaping of activist recruitment and participation: A study of women in the Mississippi civil rights movement. *Gender & Society* 12:6: 692–709.

Jacobs, Anna W. and Larry W. Isaac. 2019. Gender composition in contentious collective action: "Girl strikers" in gilded age America – harmful, helpful, or both? *Social Science History* 43: 733–763.

Jaggar, Alison. 1989. Love and knowledge: Emotion in feminist epistemology, pp. 145–487 in Alison Jaggar and Susan R. Bordo (eds.) *Gender/body/knowledge*. New Brunswick, N.J.: Rutgers University Press.

Jaschik, Scott. 2017. Judith Butler on being attacked in Brazil. *Inside Higher Ed*, November 19. https://www.insidehighered.com/news/2017/11/13/judith-butler-discusses-being-burned-effigy-and-protested-brazil

Jasper, James. M. 1998. The emotions of protest: Affective and reactive emotions in and around social movements. *Sociological Forum* 13: 394–424.

Jay, Karla. 1999. *Tales of the Lavender Menace: A memoir of liberation*. New York: Basic Books.

Jenkins, Craig. 1983. Resource mobilization theory and the study of social movements. *Annual Review of Sociology* 9:1: 527–553.

Johnson, Christen A. and K. T. Hawbaker. 2019. #MeToo: A timeline of events, *Chicago Tribune*, May 29. www.Chicago Tribune

Jordan, Ana. 2019. *The new politics of fatherhood: Men's movements and masculinities*. New York: Springer.

Kaleem, Jaweed. 2016. 'Black Lives Matter!' chants erupt as Mothers of the Movement take the stage at the DNC. *Los Angeles Times*, July 26. https://www.latimes.com/politics/la-na-dnc-mothers-of-the-movement-20160726-snap-story.html

Katzenstein, Mary F. 1990. Feminism within American institutions: Unobtrusive mobilization in the 1980s. *Signs: Journal of Culture and Society* 16 :11: 27–54.

Kauffman, L. A. 2018. *How to read a protest: The art of organizing and resistance*. Oakland, CA: University of California Press.

Kelly, Maura. 2015. Feminist identity, collective action, and individual resistance among contemporary US feminists. *Women's Studies International Forum* 48: 81–92.

Kelly, Maura. 2014. Knitting as a feminist project? *Women's Studies International Forum* 44: 133–144.

King, Deborah. 1988. Multiple jeopardy, multiple consciousness: The context of a black feminist ideology. *Signs: Journal of Culture and Society* 14 :1: 42–72.

Klawiter, Maren. 1999. Racing for the cure, walking women, and toxic touring: Mapping cultures of action within the Bay Area terrain of breast cancer. *Social Problems* 46:1: 104–126.

Klein, Ethel. 1984. *Gender politics*. Cambridge, MA: Harvard University Press.

Kretschmer, Kelsey and Kristen Barber. 2016. Men at the march: Feminist movement boundaries and men's participation in Take Back the Night and Slutwalk. *Mobilization: An International Quarterly* 21:3: 1–18.

Kristof, Nicholas and Sheryl WuDunn. 2010. *Half the sky: Turning oppression into opportunity for women worldwide*. New York: Vintage Books.

Kutz-Flamenbaum, Rachel. 2007. Code Pink, Raging Grannies, and the Missile Dick Chicks: Feminist performance activism in the contemporary anti-war movement. *NWSA Journal* 19:1: 89–105.

Kuumba, M. Bahati. 2001. *Gender and social movements*. Walnut Creek, CA: Altamira Press.

Larsson, Naomi. 2020. Feminist history and Chile's social uprising. *Toward Freedom*, September 29. https://towardfreedom.org/story/feminist-history-and-chiles-social-uprising/

Leek, Cliff and Marcus Gerke. 2020. Men's movements, pp. 447–462 in Nancy Naples (ed.) *Companion to women and gender studies*. Hoboken, N.J.: Wiley.

Levitin, Michael. 2015. The triumph of Occupy Wallstreet. *The Atlantic*, June 10. https://www.theatlantic.com/politics/archive/2015/06/the-triumph-of-occupy-wall-street/395408/

Levy, Ariel. 2005. *Female chauvinist pigs, women and the rise of raunch culture*. New York: Free Press.

Lorber, Judith. 1994. *Paradoxes of gender*. New Haven, CT: Yale University Press.

Lorde, Audre. 1997. The uses of anger, pp. 278–285 in *Looking back, moving forward: 25 years of women's studies history*. New York: The Feminist Press at the City University of New York.

Lucal, Betsy. 1999. What it means to be gendered me: Life on the boundaries of a dichotomous gender system. *Gender & Society* 13:6: 781–797.

McAdam, Doug. 1992. Gender as mediator of the activist experience: The case of Freedom Summer. *American Journal of Sociology* 97:5: 1211–1240.

McAdam, Doug. 1988. *Freedom Summer*. New York: Oxford University Press.

McAdam, Doug. 1986. Recruitment to high-risk activism: The case of Freedom Summer. *American Journal of Sociology* 92:1: 64–90.

McAdam, Doug. 1982. *Political process and the development of black insurgency*. Chicago: University of Chicago Press.

McAdam, Doug, Sidney Tarrow, and Charles Tilly. 2001. *Dynamics of contention*. New York: Cambridge University Press.

McCammon, Holly, Alison McGrath, David Hess, and Minyoung Moon. 2018. Women, leadership and the U.S. environmental movement, pp. 312–333 in Holly McCammon and Lee Ann Banaszak (eds.) *100 years of the Nineteenth Amendment: An appraisal of women's political activism*. New York: Oxford University Press.

McCammon, Holly, Karen Campbell, Ellen Granberg, and Christine Mowery. 2001. How movements win: Gendered opportunity structures and U.S. women's suffrage movements, 1866 to 1919. *American Sociological Review* 66:1: 49–70.

McCarthy, John and Mayer Zald. 1977. Resource mobilization and social movements: A partial theory. *American Journal of Sociology* 86:6:1212–1241.

McClain, Dani. 2014. The murder of Black youth is a reproductive justice issue. *Nation*, August 14. https://www.thenation.com/article/archive/murder-black-youth-reproductive-justice-issue/

Mallinson, Christine. 2017. Language and its everyday revolutionary potential: Feminist linguistic activism in the United States, pp. 419–439 in Holly McCammon, Verta Taylor, Jo Reger, and Rachel Einwohner (eds.) *The Oxford handbook of U.S. women's social movement activism*. New York: Oxford University Press.

References

Mansbridge, Jane J. 1986. *Why we lost the ERA*. Chicago: University of Chicago Press.

March on Washington, 1987. Our demands. http://www.onearchives.org/wp-content/uploads/2015/02/Our-Demands-March-on-Washington-for-Lesbian-and-Gay-Rights-Oct-11-1987.pdf

Marcus, Sara. 2010. *Girls to the front: The true story of the Riot Grrrl revolution*. New York: Harper.

Marshall, Susan E. 1985. Ladies against women: Mobilization dilemmas of antifeminist movements. *Social Problems* 32:4: 348–362.

Martin, Courtney. 2009. The end of the women's movement. *The American Prospect*, March 30. http://prospect.org/cs/articles

Martin, Patricia Yancey. 2003. "Said and done" versus "saying and doing": Gendering practices, practicing gender at work. *Gender & Society* 17:3: 342–366.

Marullo, Sam. 1991. Gender differences in peace movement participation. *Research in Social Movements, Conflict and Change* 13: 135–152.

Marullo, Sam. 1989. Gender differences in peace movement participation. Paper presented at the Eastern Sociological Association annual meetings, Baltimore, MD.

Matthews, David. 2017. Gender studies under attack from the new right. *Times Higher Education*, May 11: 11.

Matynia, Elzbieta. 2010. Polish feminism between the local and the global: A task of translation, pp. 193–228 in Amrita Basu (ed.) *Women's movements in the global era: The power of local feminisms*. Boulder, CO: Westview Press.

Melucci. Alberto. 1989. *Nomads of the present: Social movements and individual needs in contemporary society*. Philadelphia: Temple University Press.

Messner, Michael. 2016. Forks in the road of men's gender politics: Men's rights vs feminist allies. *International Journal for Crime, Justice, and Social Democracy* 5:2: 6–20.

Messner, Michael, Max A. Greenberg, and Tal Peretz. 2015. *Some men: Feminist allies and the movement to end violence against women*. New York: Oxford University Press.

Meyer, David S., and Suzanne Staggenborg. 1996. Movements, countermovements, and the structure of political opportunity. *American Journal of Sociology* 101:6: 1628–1660.

Meyer, David S. and Nancy Whittier. 1994. Social movement spillover. *Social Problems*. 41:2: 277–298.

Missile Dick Chicks. no date. Join. https://www.missiledickchicks.net/join.html

Moghadam, Valentine. 2005. *Globalizing women: Transnational feminist networks*. Baltimore, MD: Johns Hopkins University.

Morris, Aldon D. 1984. *The origins of the civil rights movement: Black communities organizing for change*. New York: Free Press.

Morris, Aldon D. and Suzanne Staggenborg. 2004. Leadership in social movements, pp. 171–196 in David Snow, Sarah A. Soule, and Hanspeter Kriesi (eds.) *The Blackwell companion to social movements*. Oxford, UK: Oxford University Press.

Mueller, Carol. 1987. Collective consciousness, identity transformation, and the rise of women in public office in the United States, pp. 89–108 in Mary F. Katzenstein and Carol M. Mueller (eds.) *The women's movements of the United States and Western Europe*. Philadelphia: Temple University Press.

Nadasen, Premilla. 2010. Expanding the boundaries of the women's movement: Black feminism and the struggle for welfare rights, pp. 168–192 in Nancy A. Hewitt (ed.) *No permanent waves: Recasting histories of U.S. feminism*. New Brunswick, N.J.: Rutgers University Press.

Naples, Nancy. 2020. The changing field of women and gender studies. Online in Nancy Naples (ed.) *Companion to women and gender studies*. Hoboken, N.J.: Wiley. https://onlinelibrary.wiley.com/doi/abs/10.1002/9781119315063.ch1

Naples, Nancy, 1998. *Grassroots warriors: Activist mothering, community work, and the war on poverty*. New York and London, UK: Routledge.

Naples, Nancy. 1992. Activist mothering: Cross generational continuity in the community work of women from low-income neighborhoods. *Gender & Society* 6: 441–463.

Nardi, Peter M. 1992. Seamless souls: An introduction to men's friendships, pp. 1–14 in Peter Nardi (ed). *Men's friendships*. Vol. 1. Newbury Park: Sage Publications.

National Coalition for Men. 2020. https://ncfm.org/

National Organization for Men Against Sexism. 2019. http://nomas.org/

Neuhouser, Kevin. 1995. "Worse than men": Gendered mobilization in an urban Brazilian squatter settlement, 1971–1991. *Gender & Society* 9:1: 38–59.

Noonan, Rita K. 1995. Women against the state: Political opportunities and collective action frames in Chile's transition to democracy." *Sociological Forum* 10:1: 81–111.

NPR. 2018. How the #Metoo movement has evolved since it began 1 year ago. *All Things Considered*, October 5. www.npr.org

O'Brien, Michelle Ester. 2019. The influence of donors on cross-class social movements: Same-sex marriage and trans rights campaigns in New York State. *Social Movement Studies*, 18:5: 586–601.

Occupy Wall Street. 2019. Facts about Occupy Wall Street. http://occupywallst.org/

One archives. 1989. "Our demands." October 11. http://www.onearchives.org/wp-content/uploads/2015/02/Our-Demands-March-on-Washington-for-Lesbian-and-Gay-Rights-Oct-11-1987.pdf

Pal, Poulomi. 2017. The Indian women's movement today: The challenges of addressing gender-based violence, pp. 129–154 in Amrita Basu (ed.) *Women's movements in the global era: The power of local feminisms*. New York: Westview Press.

Pallares, Amalia. 2015. *Family activism, immigrant struggles, and the politics of non-citizen*ship. New Brunswick, N.J.: Rutgers University Press.

Papachristou, Judith. 1976. *Women together: A history in documents of the women's movement in the United States.* New York: Alfred Knopf.

Pardo, Mary. 1998. *Mexican American women activists: Identity and resistance in two Los Angeles communities.* Philadelphia: Temple University Press.

Passy, Florence and Marco Giugni. 2001. Social networks and individual perceptions: Explaining differential participation in social movements. *Sociological Forum* 16:1: 123–153.

Payne, Charles. 1990. "Men led, but women organized": Movement participation of women in the Mississippi Delta, pp. 156–166 in Guida West and Rhonda L. Blumberg (eds.) *Women and social protest.* New York: Oxford University Press.

Pentney, Beth Ann. 2008. Feminist activism, and knitting: Are fibre arts a viable mode for feminist political action? *thirdspace: a journal of feminist theory & culture* 8:1(summer): online.

Pickerill, Jenny and John Krinsky. 2015. Why does Occupy matter? pp. 1–9 in Jenny Pickerill, John Krinsky, Graeme Hayes, Kevin Gillan, and Brian Doherty (eds.) *Occupy! A global movement.* London: Routledge.

Pike, Isabel. 2020. A discursive spectrum: The narrative of Kenya's "neglected boy child." *Gender & Society* 34:2: 284–306.

Promise Keepers. 2020. https://promisekeepers.org/

Raging Grannies International. 1987. Our philosophy. https://raginggrannies.org/philosophy/

Redden, Elizabeth. 2018. Hungary officially ends gender studies programs. *Inside Education,* October 17. www.insidehighered.com

Reger, Jo (ed.). 2019. *Nevertheless, they persisted: Feminisms and continued resistance in the U.S. women's movement.* New York: Routledge.

Reger, Jo. 2012. *Everywhere and nowhere: Contemporary feminism in the United States.* New York: Oxford University Press.

Reger, Jo. 2012a. DIY fashion and going BUST: Wearing feminist politics in the 21st century, pp. 209–225 in Shira Tarrant and Marjorie Jolles (eds.) *Fashion talks: Undressing the power of style.* Albany, N.Y.: SUNY Press.

Reger, Jo. 2004. Organizational 'emotion work' through consciousness-raising: An analysis of a feminist organization. *Qualitative Sociology* 27:2: 205–222.

Reger, Jo. 2001. Motherhood and the construction of feminist identities: Variations in a women's movement organization. *Sociological Inquiry* 71: 85–110.

Reger, Jo and Verta Taylor. 2002. Women's movement research and social movement theory: A symbiotic relationship. *Research in Political Sociology,* "Sociological views on political participation in the 21st century" 10: 85–121.

Reger, Jo, Verta Taylor, and Nancy Whittier. 1995. Gender and social movements:

Answering the call for a gender revolution. Paper presented at the American Sociological Association meetings.

Ridgeway, Cecilia. 2001. Gender, status, and leadership. *Journal of Social Issues* 57:4: 637–655.

Risman, Barbara. 2004. Gender as a social structure: Theory wrestling with activism. *Gender & Society* 18:4: 429–450.

Robinson, Christine M., and Sue E. Spivey. 2007. The politics of masculinity and the ex-gay movement. *Gender & Society* 21:5: 650–675.

Robnett, Belinda. 1997. *How long? How long? African American women in the struggle for civil rights.* New York: Oxford University Press.

Roth, Benita. 2004. *Separate roads to feminism: Black, Chicana, and white feminist movements in America's second wave.* New York: Cambridge University Press.

Rupp, Leila, Verta Taylor, and Benita Roth. 2017. Women in the lesbian, gay, bisexual, and transgender movement, pp. 664–684 in Holly McCammon, Verta Taylor, Jo Reger, and Rachel Einwohner (eds.) *The Oxford handbook of U.S. women's social movement activism.* New York: Oxford University Press.

Rupp, Leila J. and Verta Taylor. 1999. Women's culture and lesbian feminism activism: A reconsideration of cultural feminism. *Signs: Journal of Culture and Society* 19: 32–61.

Rupp, Leila and Verta Taylor. 1987. *Survival in the doldrums: The American women's rights movement, 1945 to 1960s.* New York: Oxford University Press.

Salo, Elane. 2010. South African feminisms – A coming of age? pp. 29–56 in Amrita Basu (ed.) *Women's movements in the global era: The power of local feminisms.* Boulder, CO: Westview Press.

Schilt, Kristin and Laurel Westbrook. 2015. Bathroom battlegrounds and penis panics. *Contexts*, August. https://contexts.org/articles/bathroom-battle-grounds-and-penis-panics/

Schippers, Mimi. 2002. *Rockin' out of the box: Gender maneuvering in alternative hard rock.* New Brunswick, N.J.: Rutgers University Press.

Schreiber, Ronnee. 2017. Anti-feminist, pro-life, and anti-ERA women, pp. 313–332 in Holly McCammon, Verta Taylor, Jo Reger, and Rachel Einwohner (eds.) *The Oxford handbook of U.S. women's social movement activism.* New York: Oxford University Press.

Schrock. Douglas, Daphne Holden, and Lori Reid. 2004. Creating emotional resonance: Interpersonal emotion work and motivational framing in a transgender community. *Social Problems* 51:1: 61–81.

Schussman, Alan and Earl, Jennifer., 2004. From barricades to firewalls? Strategic voting and social movement leadership in the Internet age. *Sociological Inquiry* 74:4: 439–463.

Shields, Stephanie, Dallas N. Garner, Brooke Di Leone, and Alena M. Hadley. 2006. Gender and emotion, pp. 63–83 in Jan Stets and Jonathan H. Turner (eds.) *Handbook of the sociology of emotions.* New York: Springer.

Silva, Tony. 2016. Bud-sex: Constructing normative masculinity among rural straight men that have sex with men. *Gender & Society* 31:1: 51–73.

Snortland, Ellen. 2011. Click! Go ahead, call me a bitch. https://msmagazine.com/2011/03/29/click-go-ahead-call-me-a-bitch/

Snow, David A., Louis A. Zurcher, and Sheldon Ekland-Olson. 1980. Social networks and social movements: A microstructural approach to differential recruitment. *American Sociological Review* 45:5: 787–801.

Snyder, R. Clare. 2008. Third wave feminism: A new directions essay. *Signs: A Journal of Culture and Society* 33:4 (Autumn): 175–196.

Stacey, Judith, and Barrie Thorne. 1985. The missing feminist revolution in sociology. *Social Problems* 32:4: 301–316.

Staggenborg, Suzanne and Verta Taylor. 2005. Whatever happened to the women's movement? *Mobilization: The International Journal of Research* 10:1: 37–52.

Stall, Susan, and Randy Stoecker. 1998. Community organizing or organizing community?: Gender and the crafts of empowerment. *Gender & Society* 12:6: 729–756.

Stein, Arlene. 2010. The incredible shrinking lesbian world and other queer conundra. *Sexualities* 13:1: 21–32.

Stephan, Rita. 2019. Not-so-secret weapons: Lebanese women's rights activists and extended family networks. *Social Problems* 66: 609–625.

Stone, Meghan and Rachel Vogelstein. 2019. Celebrating #MeToo's global impact. *Foreign Policy*, March 7. www.foreignpolicy.com

Stover, Kayla and Sherry Cable. 2017. American women's environmental activism: Motivations, experiences, and transformations, pp. 685–707 in Holly McCammon, Verta Taylor, Jo Reger, and Rachel Einwohner (eds.) *The Oxford handbook of U.S. women's social movement activism.* New York: Oxford University Press.

Stryker, Susan. 2017. *Transgender history: The roots of today's revolution*, 2nd edition. New York: Seal Press.

Suárez, Fátima. 2019. Identifying with inclusivity: Intersectional Chicana feminisms, pp. 25–42 in Jo Reger (ed.) *Nevertheless, they persisted: Feminisms and continued resistance in the U.S. women's movement.* New York: Routledge.

Sugiman, Pamela. 1992. "That wall's comin' down": Gendered strategies of worker resistance in the UAW Canadian Region (1963–1970). *The Canadian Journal of Sociology / Cahiers canadiens de sociologie* 17:1: 1–27.

Taft, Jessica K. 2010. *Rebel girls: Youth activism and social change across the Americas.* New York: NYU Press.

Tarrow, Sidney. 1998. *Power in movement: Social movements and contentious politics.* Cambridge, MA: Cambridge University Press.

Taub, Amanda. 2020. Mothers' power in the U.S. protests echoes a global tradition. *New York Times*, July 25. https://nyti.ms

References

Taylor, Judy. 1998. Feminist tactics and friendly fire in the Irish women's movement. *Gender & Society* 12: 6: 674–669.

Taylor, Verta. 2000. Emotions and identity in women's self-help movements, pp. 271–299 in Sheldon Striker, T. J. Owens, and R. W. White (eds.) *Self, identity and social movements*. Minneapolis: University of Minnesota.

Taylor, Verta. 1999. Gender and social movements: Gender processes in women's self-help movements. *Gender & Society* 13:1: 8–33.

Taylor, Verta. 1996. *Rock-a-by baby: Feminism, self-help and postpartum depression*. New York: Routledge.

Taylor, Verta. 1989. Sources of continuity in social movements: The women's movement in abeyance. *American Sociological Review* 54: 761–775.

Taylor, Verta, Leila J. Rupp, and Joshua Gamson. 2004. Performing protest: Drag shows as tactical repertoire of the gay and lesbian movement, pp. 105–137 in Daniel J. Myers and D. M. Cress (eds.) *Authority in contention*. Bingley: Emerald Group Publishing Limited.

Taylor, Verta and Nella Van Dyke. 2004. "Get up, stand up": Tactical repertoires of social movements, pp. 262–293 in David Snow, Sarah Soule, and Hanspeter Kriesi (eds.) *The Blackwell Companion to Social Movements*. Malden, MA: Blackwell Publishing.

Taylor, Verta, Katrina Kimport, Nella Van Dyke, and Ellen Ann Andersen. 2009. Culture and mobilization: Tactical repertoires, same-sex weddings, and the impact on gay activism. *American Sociological Review* 74:6: 865–890.

Taylor, Verta and Nancy Whittier. 1997. *The new feminist movement*, pp. 544–561 in Laurel Richardson, Verta Taylor and Nancy Whittier (eds.) *Feminist Frontiers IV*. New York: McGraw Hill.

Taylor, Verta and Nancy Whittier. 1995. Analytical approaches to social movement culture: The culture of the women's movement, pp. 163–187 in Hank Johnston and Bert Klandermans (eds.) *Social movements and culture*. Minneapolis, MN: University of Minnesota Press.

Taylor, Verta and Nancy Whittier. 1992. Collective identity in social movement communities: Lesbian feminist mobilization, pp. 104–129 in Aldon D. Morris and Carol McClurg Mueller (eds.) *Frontiers in Social Movement Theory*. New Haven and London: Yale University Press.

Thomas, Jan. 1999. Everything about us is feminist: The significance of ideology in organizational change. *Gender & Society* 13: 101–119.

Thompson, Becky. 2002. Multiracial feminism: Recasting the chronology of second wave feminism. *Feminist Studies* 28: 337–663.

Thorne, Barrie. 1975. Protest and the problem of credibility: Uses of knowledge and risk-taking in the draft resistance movement of the 1960s. *Social Problems* 23:2: 111–123.

Tilly, Charles. 1978. *From mobilization to revolution*. Cambridge, UK: Cambridge University Press.

Travers, Ann. 2018. *The trans generation: How trans kids (and their parents) are creating a gender revolution*. New York: NYU Press.

Tripp, Aili Mari. 2017. Women's movements in Africa, pp. 37–64 in Amrita Basu (ed.) *Women's movements in the global era: The power of local feminisms*. New York: Westview Press.

Upton, Aisha and Joyce Bell. 2017. Women's activism in the modern movement for Black liberation, pp. 623–642 in Holly McCammon, Verta Taylor, Jo Reger, and Rachel Einwohner (eds.) *The Oxford handbook of U.S. women's social movement activism*. New York: Oxford University Press.

Vidal-Ortiz, Salvador. 2020. Transgender movements, online in Nancy Naples (ed.) *Companion to women and gender studies*. Hoboken, N.J.: Wiley. https://onlinelibrary.wiley.com/doi/abs/10.1002/9781119315063.ch1

Walters, Suzanna Danuta. 2014. *The tolerance trap: How God, genes, and good intentions are sabotaging gay equality*. New York, NYU Press.

Weiss, Jillian Todd. 2009. Teaching transgender issues: Global social movements based on gender identity. *Counterpoints, A twenty-first century approach to teaching social justice: Educating for both advocacy and action* 358: 27–38.

West, Candace and Don Zimmerman. 1987. Doing gender. *Gender & Society* 1:2: 125–151.

Westbrook, Laurel and Kristen Schilt. 2013. Doing gender, determining gender: Transgender people, gender panics and the maintenance of the sex/gender/sexuality system. *Gender & Society* 28:1: 32–57.

White Ribbon Campaign. 2020. https://www.whiteribbon.ca/

Whittier, Nancy. 2019. Activism against sexual assault on campus: Origins, opportunities and outcomes, pp. 133–150 in Jo Reger (ed.) *Nevertheless, they persisted: Feminisms and continued resistance in the U.S. women's movement*. New York: Routledge.

Whittier, Nancy. 2009. *The politics of child sexual abuse: Emotion, social movements and the state*. New York: Oxford University Press.

Whittier, Nancy, 2007. Gender and social movements, pp. 1872–1875 in George Ritzer (ed.) *The Blackwell encyclopedia of sociology*, vol. IV. Maiden, MA: Blackwell Publishing.

Whittier, Nancy. 2001. Emotional strategies: The collective reconstruction and display of oppositional emotions in the movement against child sexual abuse, pp. 233–250 in Francesca Polletta, Jeff Goodwin, and James Jasper (eds.) *Political passions: Emotions and social movements*. Chicago: University of Chicago Press.

Whittier, Nancy. 1995. *Feminist generations: The persistence of the radical women's movement*. Philadelphia: Temple University Press.

Wilson, Ara. 2007. Feminism in the space of the World Social Forum. *Journal of International Women's Studies* 8:3: 10–27.

Winerip, Michael. 2009. Where to pass the torch. *New York Times*, March 8. http://nytimes.com/2009/03/08/fashion/08generationb.html

References

Wolf, Naomi. 1990. *The beauty myth: How images of beauty are used against women.* New York: Chatto & Windus.

WoLF. no date. A statement of principles. http://womensliberationfront.org/document-statement-of-principles/

Index

Abelson, Miriam, 148
abortion, 8, 31, 160; abortion boat, 133
Acker, Joan, 6
activism: Black activists, 61, 67, 90–94, 118, 132; cycles of protest, 11; default activist, 26, 31, 80, 117, 140, 142, 177; intersectionality, 12–13, 25, 34–35, 50–52, 68, 76, 80, 91, 102, 104; Wall of Dads, 73, 99–100, 184n3; Wall of Moms, 73, 96, 99, 103, 133–134, 184n3. *See also* social movements
activist gender stereotypes, 60–68, 74–75, 80; default activist, 26, 31, 80, 117, 140, 142; gendered activists, 62–68; race, 61; sex, 60–61; sexual identity, 61–62, 97–104
Adams, Jacqueline, 66
alt-right movements, 72–73
American Prospect, 158
American Psychiatric Association's Diagnostic and Statistical Manual of Mental Disorders (DSM), 152
anger, 106, 108
animal rights campaigns, 103–104
anti-nuclear movement, 71–72
anti-violence campaigns, 46
anti-war movements, 70–72, 132
Appalachian women, 62–64

Argentina, 97–98, 107, 108, 170–171, 184n5
Australia, 108

Bachelet, Michele, 39
backlash, 156–69; intellectual, 164–166; mainstream, 157–160; popular, 164–166; social countermovements, 160–164; women's movement, 32–33
Baker, Carrie, 79
Baker, Ella, 118
Barber, Kristen, 46
Barnett, Bernice McNair, 118
Basu, Amrita, 173
beauty myth, 24
Beckwith, Karen, 60
Beijing conference Platform of Action, 37
Bell, Shannon Elizabeth, 63
Bergstrand, Kelly, 88
Beyerlein, Kraig, 87, 88
binary identities, 4, 25–27, 167, 178–179; breaking down, 146–153; gendered emotion, 104–111, 113
Black activists, 61, 67, 90–94, 132; women leaders, 118
Black Lives Matter Global Network Foundation, Inc., 84
Black Lives Matter movement, 11, 33, *83,* 83–84, 84–88, 90, 109, 132; identity outside the

movement, 103; intersectionality, 102; Portland, 96; Wall of Dads, 73, 99–100, 184n3; Wall of Moms, 73, 96, 99, 103, 133–134, 184n3
Black women's club movement, 28
Blee, Kathy, 64, 75
Bosco, Fernando, 97
bra burners, 23
Brazil, 97, 165–166
breast cancer walkathons, 138–139
Bridges, Tristan, 47–48, 49, 51
bud sex, 5
Burke, Tarana, 3
Butler, Judith, 165–166

Cable, Sherry, 87
Caldicott, Helen, 63, 64
Canada, 45–46
Cappelli, Mary, 106–107, 108
Casa Ruby, 155
Catholic Church, 33, 139–140
Chan, Jody, 70
Chappell, Bill, 144
Chauvin, Derek, 109
Chemaly, Soraya, 106
Chile, 37–41, 66, 80, 130–131
Chinese Exclusion Act (1882), 28, 184n1
Christopher Street Liberation Day, 152
cisgender, 4
civil disobedience, 122–123
Civil Rights Movement, 55, 55–59, 66, 76–77, 118, 184n2
class issues, 12, 89, 102
Code Pink, 124–125, 132
community organizing, 117–118
Compton Cafeteria Riot, 151
Connell, Raewyn, 44–45, 49, 69, 71
contentious politics movement, 11
Cooper, Brittney, 106
Corpora en Libertad, 155
Crenshaw, Kimberlé, 93
Curnow, Joe, 70
cycles of protest, 11

Davis, Heath, 154–155
default activist, 26, 31, 80, 117, 140, 142, 177
Dobie, Kathy, 160
doing emotion, 105
doing gender, 4–5, 147
drag queens, 151–152, 172

Earl, Jennifer, 9–10
Echols, Alice, 24, 77
Einwohner, Rachel, 74, 103–104, 105, 106, 181
El/la Trans Latina, 155
El Poder Femenino, 38
emotion: doing emotion, 105; emotional expression as gendered strategy, 128–129; emotional socialization, 109; gender and, 104–111; in graffiti, 107, 108
Empire Pride Agenda, 153
Enloe, Cynthia, 181–182
Ensler, Eve, 149
environmental movement, 63, 89, 94
Equal Rights Amendment (ERA), 28, 32, 161–164
Evans, Leisha, 132
expertise, 70

Faludi, Susan, 159–160
family, nuclear, 145
Farrell, Warren: *The Liberated Man,* 43; *The Myth of Male Power,* 44–45
fathers' rights organizations, 51
Feinberg, Leslie, 147
femininity reclaimed, 139–140
feminism. *See* Women's movement
Ferree, Myra Marx, 36, 95
Floyd, George, 83, 83–84, 96, 107, 108, 109
Fonow, Mary Margaret, 115
frames and counter-frames, 92–96; gendered frames, 93–96
Freedom Summer (1964), 55, 55–59, 66, 76–77, 80; interracial relationships, 77
Freeman, Jo, 89, 90

Index

Friedan, Betty, 30
friendly fire, 70

Galli, Anya, 134–135
Gandhi, Mahatma, 122
Garrison, Ednie Kaeh, 159
Garza, Alicia, 84, 90, 102–103
gender: binary, 4, 7; cisgender, 4; class issues and, 12, 89, 102; definitions, 4; emotions and, 104–111; gender studies, 165; gender *versus* sex, 3; gendered frames, 93–96; gendered mobilization, 96–97; gendered strategies, 9–10, 122–129; gendered tactics, 8–10, 129–140; leadership issues and, 115–122, 172; multi-gender movements, 55–113; networks, 91; as performance, 4–5, 137; power and, 180; race issues and, 12, 102; relevancy in social movements, 173–175; risk and, 71, 73–74, 88; shaping social change, 114–142, 143–169; shifting gender norms, 79–80; social structures and gender, 175–176; stratification, 3–4, 176–178; in structures, 6; transgressions of norms, 132, 172; as way of sorting society, 3–7
Gender and Social Movements (Reger): organization of book, 16–19
gender fluid, 4
gender maneuvering, 5
gender non-binary, 4
gender non-conforming, 4
gender panics, 5
gender scholarship, 180; integrating, 13–15
Gerber, Lynne, 136
Gerke, Marcus, 72–73
Gerson, Judith, 14
Goldberg, Herb, 43
Goodwin, Jeff, 107
graffiti, 107, 108
Grandmothers (Abuelas) of Plaza de Mayo. *See* Madres de Plaza de Mayo
Gutiérrez, Jennicet, 153, 154

Hairgrove, Frank, 74
Hands Across the Aisle, 150
hashtags, 11. *See also* frames and counter-frames
Hawkesworth, Mary, 33
Hay, Harry, 77
Hayden, Casey, 59, 61
Heath, Melanie, 50
hegemonic masculinity, 49
Hercus, Cheryl, 105, 108
hierarchy, 117
Hill, Anita, 107
Hipp, John R., 87
Hochschild, Arlie, 42, 123, 177
homophile movement, 77
homophobia, 41, 51
Honey, Michael, 76
Humienny, Cecelia, 114–116, 129
Hungary, 165
Hurwitz, Heather, 120
Hussey, Rebecca, 106
hybrid masculinity, 49
hyperfemininity, 23–24

identity, 97–104; collective, 101–102; constructed, 100; identity movements, 164; lesbian feminists, 100; outside the movement, 103; protector identity, 63; sexual identity, 61–62, 97–104; tactics and, 130, 172. *See also* binary identities
immigrant rights movement, 67–68
India, 36, 122
inequality, 15
institutional order, 6–7
internet, 9, 33–34, 111; e-movements, 10; message boards, 73
interracial relationships, 77
intersectionality, 12–13, 25, 34–35, 68, 80, 91, 181; animal rights campaigns, 104; global perspective, 181–182; identity and, 102; men's movements and, 50–52, 76
intersex people, 150
Irish feminist movement, 60, 82

Irons, Jenny, 66
Iturriaga, Nicole, 171

Jaggar, Alison, 105
Jasper, James, 107
Jay, Karla, 23
Johnson, Marsha P., 151, 152
Jordan, Ana, 41–42, 46, 48

Katzenstein, Mary, 33, 139–140
Kenya, 43–44
Khan-Cullors, Patrisse, 84, 90
King, Mary, 59, 61
Klawiter, Maren, 138
Kretschmer, Kelsey, 46
Krinsky, John, 108–109
Kristof, Nicholas, 173
Kutz-Flamenbaum, Rachel, 124–128,
    136–137
Kuumba, M. Bahati, 182

labor unions, 76, 114–115;
    leadership, 115–116
language issues, 31
Las Tesis, 39
Latinas, 67–68; Chicana feminists, 32;
    El/la Trans Latina, 155; *El Poder
    Femenino,* 38; Madres (Abuelas)
    de Plaza de Mayo, 97–98, 107,
    108, *170,* 170–172, 181, 184n5;
    transgender, 153, 155
leadership: Black women leaders,
    118; gender and, 115–122; invisible
    vs. bridge, 119, 121; stereotypes,
    120–121. *See also* default activist
Lebanon, 91
Leek, Cliff, 72–73
Levy, Ariel, 158
LGBTQ+ movement, 8, 62, 77–78,
    80, 100, 134–135, 143–145; binary
    identities, 178–179; breaking down
    binary identities, 146–153; coming
    out, 110; gay marriage, 143–145;
    Supreme Court decision of 2015,
    143–144; *Time Magazine, 143*;
    transgender and, 151–153, 172
Lorber, Judith, 3

Lorde, Audre, 106
Lucal, Betsy, 147

Madres de Plaza de Mayo, 97–98,
    107, 108, *170,* 170–172, 181,
    184n5
Mallinson, Christine, 31
March on Washington (1987),
    143–144
Marches of the Empty Pots,
    130–131
Marshall, Susan, 161–162
Martin, Patricia Yancey, 182–183
Martin, Trayvon, 84, 102
Marullo, Sam, 63, 71–72
masculinity, 48–50, 135–138; alt-right
    movements, 72–73; dignity and
    race, 76; ethnic, 75; expertise, 70;
    godly masculinity, 136; hegemonic
    masculinity, 49; invisible, 69–70;
    men as warriors, 70–79; multi-
    gender movements, 68–79; risky
    behavior, 71, 73–74, 88. *See also*
    men's movements
Mattachine Society, 77
McAdam, Doug, 13, 56–57, 60, 66,
    69, 71, 73, 116
McCammon, Holly, 25–26
McClain, Dani, 94
McCleod, Douglas, 74
Memphis Sanitation Workers' Strike
    (1968), *75, 76*
Men as Partners Network, 50
men's movements, 41–52, 99–100,
    135–138, 174; critical men's
    movement, 50; emotions of men,
    111; gay men, 51; global, 50–52;
    intersectionality, 50–52; men's
    rights, 42–45; pro-feminist, 46–48.
    See also masculinity
Messner, Michael, 41–46, 174
MeToo movement, 1–3, 16, 106,
    173
Mexico, 35
Meyer, David, 137–138
Michigan Womyn's Music Festival,
    149

Index

Milano, Alyssa, 2
military, 33, 139–140
Miss America pageant, 22, 22–25, 35, 118
Missile Dick Chicks, 126, 126–127, 132, 136–137
Morris, Aldon, 92
motherhood, 39, 65–67, 93–94, 96, 97–98, 107; Mothers of the Movement, 110; postpartum depression, 108; race and, 67–68; Wall of Moms, 96, 99, 103, 133–134, 184n3
Mothers of East Los Angeles (MELA), 67–68
Mothers of the Plaza de Mayo, 97. See Madres de Plaza de Mayo
Mott, Lucretia, 27
Mount Holyoke college, 150
Ms., 31
Mueller, Carol, 36
multi-gender movements, 55–113; activist gender stereotypes, 60–68; alt-right movements, 72–73; gender inequality in Freedom Summer, 57–59; masculinity, 68–79
Muslim men, 74

Naples, Nancy, 165
National Association of Colored Women, 28
National Coalition for Men (NCFM), 45
National Organization for Men against Sexism (NOMAS), 45–46
National Women's Party, 28, 99
networks, gendered, 89–92
Neuhouser, Kevin, 96–97
New Left, 30, 35
New York Radical Women, 23–24
New York Times, 158
Nigeria, 10
Nineteenth Amendment, 28
Noonan, Rita, 38, 131
NOW (National Organization of Women), 65; consciousness raising groups, 109–110

Obama, Barack, 154
O'Brien, Michelle, 152–153
Occupy Wall Street, 11, 109, 119–122
opportunity structures, 11

Pankhurst, Emmeline, 127
Pascoe, C. J., 49
Payne, Charles, 118
peace movement, 63–64, 137–138
Peiss, Kathy, 14
penis panics, 184n4
Pickerill, Jenny, 108–109
Pike, Isabel, 43
Pinochet, Augusto, 38–39
Poland, 88
Polletta, Francesca, 107
Portland, Oregon, 96, 133
postpartum depression, 108
power, 180
presidential election of 2000, 9
Promise Keepers, 45, 50
Protect Our Women (POW), 163
protector identity, 63
Proud Boys, 72

queer theory, 154

race: class issues and, 12, 102; dignity, 76; gender issues and, 3, 12; interracial relationships, 77; masculinity and, 76; motherhood and, 67–68
Race for the Cure, 138–139
radical feminism, 30–31
RAGE (Riders Against Gender Exclusion), 154–155
Raging Grannies, 124–126, 125, 132
Raiford, Teressa, 133
Raymond, Janice, 149
resource mobilization theory, 11
Riot Grrrl, 158
Risman, Barbara, 6
Ritchie, Andrea J., 93
Rivera, Sylvia, 151, 152, 172
Robnett, Belinda, 107, 119
Roe v. Wade, 31
Rogers, Taylor, 76

Roth, Benita, 35
Roth, Silke, 95
Rupp, Leila, 99

Salo, Elaine, 50
Sarria, José, 152
Scarboro, Lorelei, 62, 63
Schippers, Mimi, 5
Schlit, Kristen, 5
Schrock, Douglas, 109
Schussman, Alan, 9–10
Schutt, Jane, 92
Seneca Falls Women's Rights
    Convention, 27–28
sex categories, 3–4
sexual harassment, 107
Shields, Stephanie, 105
Silva, Tony, 5
SNCC, 177–178
social countermovements, 32–33,
    160–164
social justice movements, 154–156
social media, 111. *See also* internet
social movement spillover, 137
social movements: civil rights
    movement, 55, 55–59, 66,
    76–77; definitions, 8; emotion
    and, 104–111; gender relevancy,
    173–175; gendered networks,
    89–92; gendered strategies,
    9–10, 122–129; gendered tactics,
    8–10, 129–140, 172; goals, 145;
    identity and, 97–104; influences,
    176–178; intersection with gender,
    3; leadership, 115–122; men's
    movements, 41–52; mobilizations,
    96–97; multi-gender movements,
    55–113; pathways to, 83–113;
    personal availability to, 86–89;
    recruitment, 85–86; single-gender
    concerns, 22–54; social change and,
    3, 7–11, 15–16, 114–142, 143–169;
    social justice movements, 154–156;
    women's movements, 27–41
social networks, 89–92
social structures and gender, 175–176
socialists, 31

South Africa, 36
Southeastern Pennsylvania
    Transportation Authority (SEPTA),
    154–155
Stacey, Judith, 13
Staggenborg, Suzanne, 180
Stall, Susan, 117
Stanton, Elizabeth Cady, 27
STAR (Street Transvestite Action
    Revolutionaries), 151–152
Stephan, Rita, 91
stereotypes: activist gender
    stereotypes, 60–68, 74–75; naive
    white girls, 79
Stoecker, Randy, 117
Stoller, Debbie, 139
Stonewall Riot, 151
Stryker, Susan, 146, 149
Student Non-Violent Coordinating
    Committee (SNCC), 57, 59, 91,
    177–178
Suárez, Fátima, 102
suffragists, 26, 28, 94, 161
Sugiman, Pamela, 123
Supreme Court decision of 2015,
    143–144

Take Back the Night March, 46, 130,
    134
Taylor, Judy, 60, 70, 82, 133
Taylor, Verta, 14, 65, 93, 97, 99, 100,
    108, 129, 132, 180
TERF's (trans-exclusionary radical
    feminists), 150
Thomas, Clarence, 107
Thompson, Becky, 35
Thorne, Barry, 13, 71
Thunberg, Greta, 89
Time Magazine, 143; Person of the
    Year, 2
Title IX, 31, 44
Traister, Rebecca, 106
transgender movement, 109,
    146–153; feminism and, 148–151;
    LGBTQ+ movement and, 151–153;
    social justice and, 154–156
Transgender Nation, 154 ·

Travers, Ann, 146, 155
Trump, Donald, 2, 89, 154

U. S. women's movements, 27–34;
  backlash, 32–33; Black feminists
  and, 12–13; "death" of, 33; history
  in U.S., 27–34, 157–158; radical
  feminists, 30–31; socialists, 31;
  women's marches, 33. *See also*
  Women's movements
"Un Violador en tu Camino," 39
United Auto Workers, 123
United Kingdom, 41–52, 99
United Nations world conferences on
  women, 37
universal womanhood, 12

Vagina Monologues, 149–150
Van Dyke, Nella, 129, 132
victimization, 79
Vidal-Ortiz, Salvador, 152
voting campaigns, 55–59. *See also*
  suffragists

"Walk a Mile in Her Shoes," 46–48,
  47
Wall of Dads, 73, 99–100, 184n3
Wall of Moms, 73, 96, 103, 133–134,
  184n3
Walters, Suzanna Danuta, 145
Weinstein, Harvey, 2, 6–7, 39
Wells, Ida B., 28, 118

West, Candace, 4–5
Westbrook, Laurel, 5
Wheeling-Pittsburgh Steel, *114,*
  114–115, 122, 124, 129
White Ribbon campaign, 45–46, 48,
  50
Whittier, Nancy, 14, 78, 97, 100, 110,
  128–129, 137–138
WoLF (Women's Liberation Front),
  150
Wolf, Naomi, 24
Woman's March (2017-2018), 33,
  173
Women's movements, 8, 122–135;
  backlash, 32–33; Black feminists
  and, 12–13; "death" of, 33,
  157–158; femininity reclaimed,
  139–140; global, 36–41; history
  in U.S., 27–34, 157–158; radical
  feminists, 30–31; socialists, 31;
  transgender and, 148–151; women's
  marches, 33, 173. *See also* social
  movements
WuDunn, Sheryl, 173

Yellow Creek Concerned Citizens
  (YCCC), 87
Young, Aurelia, 66

Zimbabwe, 88
Zimmerman, Don, 4–5
Zimmerman, George, 84